THE GREAT BOHUNKUS

The Great Bohunkus

TRIBUTES TO IAN MACKAY

EDITED BY
Trevor Evans

WITH A FOREWORD BY
LORD BEAVERBROOK

W. H. ALLEN
LONDON
1953

*Made and printed in Great Britain by
The Garden City Press Ltd., Letchworth, Herts,
for the publishers,
W. H. Allen & Co., Ltd.,
43 Essex Street, London, W.C.2*

Contents

Contents

List of Illustrations

The drawing between pages 104 and 105 of Walter Duranty and Ian Mackay in Fleet Street is by Ivan Opffer, the American cartoonist.

Foreword

BY

LORD BEAVERBROOK

Ian, the man of no rancour

IAN MACKAY was a wit who took pleasure in the wit of others; an erudite man who took no pride in his own scholarship; a man of deep convictions and no rancour. He was also a winsomely human personality who had the gift of transmitting his gaiety into *News Chronicle* columns. In consequence, many thousands of people who never set eyes on Ian became acquainted with his staunch and humorous character.

But we in Fleet Street knew him best, and this is a book of Fleet Street memories.

Fleet Street concedes its respect to men who display high professional ability in one section or another of the trade of newspapers. But it gives its love rarely and on a different principle.

Ian Mackay was loved by his fellow-craftsmen not because he was—as he was—a journalist of talent and even of genius, but because he had all the qualities which many journalists admire and had them to an exceptional degree. He was Bohemian and boisterous. He was a mirror in which other men saw themselves, if not as they were at any rate as they would like to be—and somewhat enlarged.

He was also a reminder of the glorious truth that there is no approved path to success in journalism. He had broken into Fleet Street, like a genial burglar, from the Far North by an unconventional route. He began his working life as a chemist's assistant. It is not a bad place to start.

But those who were conscious only of the gay and wayward side of his character would have missed what was its most important ingredient. He was a serious journalist who had prepared for his career by taking a course at London University. He was also a man of deep and strong convictions in politics.

One conviction alone was stronger than any of them: his immense and contagious affection for human beings, no matter how wildly wrong he thought their opinions. This emerged clearly as many a long, jovial and controversial evening passed. Ian would talk passionately, even with indignation. But there was no Tory whose views he denounced, no Communist whose philosophy he detested, but found in him a man and a brother. This gift made him, in an age of many great journalists, the uncrowned king of his profession, chosen by the irresistible franchise of friendship.

When Ian came into a room it grew smaller and warmer. And when, far too soon, he left Fleet Street, it became a poorer and sadder place. How rich it was, however, in memories of a good man! Some of them, recorded in the pages that follow by men who were his close companions, will convey to a wider public and preserve to a later age the essence of this rare and gifted Scotsman.

Look on this as a book in which Fleet Street takes pride in one of its own.

Grub Street

A Song for Ian Mackay

In Grub Street may be worms and moles
Who delve and snuffle through the night
In print-black alleys by St. Bride's
With tales that never see the light:
And there are noble souls.

Where Samuel Johnson stomped along
Are prophets shrill with inky lips
Who feed the night with policy
And dark advice and racing tips:
And there are men of song.

O east of Temple Bar the street
Gleams bright with luck and muck and gold.
Dreaming on desks or tavern stools
Are fools who know that life is sweet,
And men who won't be sold.

Bouverie Street and Dorset Rise
Slope down to the tides of the sea,
And the soulful sigh for wider worlds,
Cramming their worlds to column size.
But souls, there are, range free.

Where Grub Street ends beneath St. Paul's
And trains puff up their cloudy prayers
Are men who raise a glass and tell
How the world wags within four walls.
But the wide world is theirs.

JOHN PUDNEY.

11

Editor's Note

ONE of the barred words in most newspaper offices is "unique." So few things are unique. So few words invite such overwork.

Let us be content, therefore, to claim that this volume is unusual. For all the contributors to it, writers and artists, have freely donated these recollections of Ian Mackay, an outstanding newspaperman of this generation, a man whose warm heart had no room for envy or rancour, and whose companionship was an inspiration to all who enjoyed it.

Great though our grief was at his passing at 54, there is little sorrow in this book. Indeed, the dominant feeling in our hearts is gratitude to Ian Mackay for the many happy hours he gave us, and for the cheerful memories he bequeathed us.

The men who have written and illustrated this book come from many newspaper offices. That is unusual, too—and significant. For although Ian Mackay worked for these last twenty years for the *News Chronicle*, the whole of Fleet Street felt he belonged to the Street.

It is partly to recall our own association with Ian Mackay, and partly to share our pleasure with the thousands who knew him not, that this tribute has been compiled.

Nor do we intend that this shall be all. There has been established the Ian Mackay Memorial Fund, administered by trustees elected by the London Press Club to help newspapermen who fall on bad times. The whole proceeds of this book after meeting the cost of its production will go to this Fund.

Thus the enthusiastic response of the contributors is backed by the generous co-operation of Mr. Mark Goulden, representing the publishers, and Mr. Frank Betts, our literary agent.

I must, too, express publicly my gratitude to Mr. John S. Mather, Revise Editor of the *Daily Express*, for his brilliant technical preparation of the work ("subbing" to newspapermen), and to Mrs. Rosemary Mackay, Mr. Hugh Chevins, of the *Daily Telegraph*, for their constant availability for helpful consultation, and Miss Jean Stannard, who showed uncanny skill in deciphering contributors' handwriting!

No nickname ever fitted a man as comfortably as the Great Bohunkus fitted Ian Mackay. It probably started as a taunt. It blossomed into a *nom de cœur*. If Mackay had lived long enough to be jollied into writing his autobiography its title assuredly would have been this.

There is doubt as to who first applied it. Some say Tom Innes, a merry and erudite Fleet Street philosopher: others Ronald Walker, often uncannily perceptive in his spontaneous descriptions; still others name Vivian Brodzky, who had worked in the strangest variety of callings along the coast of British Columbia and California, where the name "Bohunk" was commonly and derisively applied to shiftless and moonstruck immigrants from Southern and Middle Europe, including Bohemia. Yes, Bohemia. And if ever a man belonged to the Bohemia of the soul it was Ian Mackay.

That word-lover Mackay was quick to relish the full rotundity of the Latinised version of Bohunk, and shrewd enough to appreciate the variety of roles conjured by its sound. The adjective added to it, and accepted by Mackay without any immodesty, helped to create the vision of a magician or a florid ring-master in the Circus of Life.

Sometimes, in moments of exaggerated mock-pomposity, he would refer to himself as The Great Bohunkus. Indeed, he had it engraved below his own name on a tankard he presented to the Press Club.

We, his intimates, accepted the name as placidly as if it had been written in, whimsically, on his birth certificate. All this has been a secret of the few for twenty years and more. And now we share it.

TREVOR EVANS.

London, July 1953.

PART ONE

The Magnetism of
Ian Mackay

BY

TREVOR EVANS

*Industrial Correspondent of the " Daily Express" ; former chairman of
the Industrial Correspondents' Group; founder and first honorary treasurer
of the Ian Mackay Memorial Fund.*

A**BOUT** once in every generation a man becomes a
legend in Fleet Street. There is something very special
about that. For nowhere is this accolade awarded with
greater reluctance, with more professional and instinctive
scrutiny, than in the crowded parish where the country's
national newspapers are nightly born.

Legendary status came to Ian Mackay—John Cockburn
Marshall Mackay—because he hated convention and
because he was an instinctive perfectionist. He had many
other qualities, comradeship and kindliness being the most
obvious. But it was his utter contempt for the conventional
in the years of his establishment as an unusual personality
which made Fleet Street and then the wider world realise
that this "wild boy from Wick" was a natural Bohemian.

Here was no smooth pebble tossed into the pool of Fleet
Street. Here was a jagged rock, causing ripples which sprinted
to the shores of the most somnolent backwaters. He captivated me from the moment he sought me out in a modest
Glasgow hotel lounge one Easter Sunday evening in the
early 'thirties to tell me that from the next day he would be
the Industrial Correspondent of the *News Chronicle*.

He was travelling south from Stirling, where he had been a delegate to a journalists' conference, and had broken his journey at Glasgow because, from my newspaper, he had seen that I was in the city attending a Co-operative Party Conference.

"Thought I'd drop in to make myself known to you," he murmured. Then he added, with a twinkle, "Also thought it wouldn't be a bad idea to measure what my opposition is like." I at once offered him a copy of the story I had sent earlier that evening for publication in my newspaper next morning. Hastily he said, "No, thanks—I don't start officially until tomorrow. No good showing too much anxiety." This struck me as odd and ominous. Here, I thought, is a man who stands by the letter of his contract. No work beyond that specified in his agreement.

My companion was Jack Juster, of the Press Association, a balanced and perceptive colleague. I asked him later, "What do you make of this Mackay? Isn't it curious that he should be so reluctant to pass on a story to his paper, which isn't represented here?" Jack, who had known Mackay in the parliamentary lobby, said carefully, "Take it from me, Ian knows what he's about." And how well Ian knew what he was about I was to see for myself before the night was over.

It was after eleven o'clock when Jack Juster and I returned to our hotel and there was Mackay, surrounded by a group of Co-operative Party leaders, including A. V. (now Lord) Alexander. They were all in right good mood. Gusts of laughter exploded from the company. Mackay was talking. Mackay had also been learning—learning about the decisions the Co-ops had reached in their two days of conference, learning the political implications of those decisions. He was already an artist in leading people to talk about their own interests. It needed skill in those circles at that time, for the Co-ops were deeply suspicious of talking to newspapermen on "capitalist" journals. Nor had Mackay the advantage of knowing any of them, except A. V. Alexander, whom he had met in the lobbies of Parliament.

Within minutes of us joining the party, Ian, with a toss of his untamed black mop of hair and a wink, indicated that I should follow him, and he stalked from the lounge into the retiring room. There I found him in a state of suppressed excitement. He said, "I didn't see the copy you offered me, but these chaps have explained what it all means, and it's pretty lively." From Mackay the whole story came out. It not only confirmed but amplified my earlier conclusions. And my report next day was greatly improved by Ian's contribution.

That was how our association began. There never was a more unrestrained sharer of information than Mackay—nor a more appreciative recipient. There was nothing secretive about him. In his professional relations his own candour was so bountiful that reciprocity was inevitable.

Yet, this very quality caused the first criticism of Ian Mackay I ever heard. Shortly after returning to London from Glasgow I introduced Ian to John Scanlon, then a colleague of mine, a brilliant, bitter man, whose acid tongue and sarcastic pen caused many to keep their distance from him. Two of his books, *Very Foreign Affairs* and *Pillars of Cloud*, had made most of the Labour Party leaders his sworn enemies. Scanlon had been a riveter in a Glasgow shipyard before he entered politics as a militant member of the old Independent Labour Party. He had been secretary to John Wheatley and Sir Patrick Hastings before catching the eye and interest of Lord Beaverbrook, who engaged him as a Labour correspondent. John, a reserved man, spoke so quietly that you had to bend close to hear him. Except when he was angry. Then he would hiss his wounding words. But I liked and respected John for his knowledge and integrity.

One evening Scanlon called on me to join him in a drink

as he had something important to tell me. In the pub John looked contemplatively into his whisky as if pondering how to phrase his *pronunciamiento*. Then he looked me squarely in the eyes, and declared solemnly, "Yon Mackay's a poseur." I looked at John incredulously and demanded an amplification. He hissed, "You see yon mirror at the back of the bar? Last night I caught him primping in it, and he rearranged his hair to look even more unruly than usual. Mark my words, he's doing it to attract attention to himself. It's the same with the cuffs of his coat. He keeps them ragged on purpose. It's a pose."

Now John Scanlon felt deeply about politics and poverty. He couldn't have been professionally jealous of Mackay because Scanlon regarded himself more as a consultant on political and economic trends than as a journalist. But I was convinced that Scanlon had a deeper reason for criticising Ian than any objection to his hair or cuffs. Come to think of it, John, though a neat dresser, was no dandy.

"Tell me more, John," I urged. It took a lot of prodding and wheedling to get at the back of the complicated Scanlon mind. Then it all came out in a rush.

Scanlon, it seemed, had given Ian an exclusive story of an important development in Socialist Party policy. It was Scanlon's intention that only two newspapers, his own and Ian's, should publish the story. But it had appeared in four newspapers the following morning. Ian had met two other journalists from different newspapers on his way back to his office, and with his usual impulsiveness had told them the story without consulting Scanlon. And hence Scanlon's anger tortuously concentrated on Mackay's hair and cuffs! Appropriately it was this breezy talkativeness of Mackay's which, a few months later, won Scanlon's forgiveness and admiration.

It was at a Hampstead party given to celebrate the

intention of a mettlesome young peer to join the Labour Party. The operative word is *intention*. The peer was getting tipsy, and the tipsier he got the greater honour he felt he was bestowing on the Labour Party. He started to boast, to the embarrassment of his host and fellow-guests, that his line of descent went back uninterruptedly for nearly six centuries. "There's a shock coming for some of my forbears," he declared. Quicker and quicker the chatter went on around him in a gallant attempt to smother his indiscretion. The young peer felt aggrieved. He looked around for an audience. He saw Ian Mackay and weaved towards him. He steadied himself, and flicking Ian across the lapel, he repeated piercingly so that all could hear, "I was just saying that my line goes back to the fourteenth century. How far back can you go?"

Ian stiffened his six feet and resonantly replied, "Sir, eighteen ninety-eight; I was born out of wedlock."

Most of the guests prided themselves on their broadmindedness, but they gasped. The young peer staggered into a corner never to mingle in that company again. Ian himself stood more erect than he had ever done during his army training in the first world war. It was Scanlon who broke the tension by blurting out admiringly, "Mon, that was a bonny and telling retort." Ian bowed with a curiously awkward dignity, and the party went on cheerfully.

Mackay had not referred to his mother. He rarely did. There were depths of devotion which even the discursive Mackay refused to plumb. And he was infinitely devoted to that remarkable woman, Jessie Mackay, domestic servant. With her hard-earned pence she accumulated a library of more than 3,000 classics for her three sons, of whom Ian was the eldest. Ian's father, Angus Mackay, engine-driver on the Highland Railway, had died from an accident on the line which pitchforked him into a haystack.

The Magnetism of Ian Mackay

Once, years later, when Ian was an honoured guest at the home of a distinguished Cambridge don, he permitted the world one furtive peep into the storehouse of his fragrant memories of his mother. It was Christmas, 1948. He wrote: "Christmas at Cambridge was pure delight. I stayed at Girton in a lovely house filled with beautiful books which 'Q,' Gilbert Murray and 'The Shropshire Lad' had handled, and pianos in every room which have thrilled to the touch of Honegger, Kodaly, Alban Berg and the great Vaughan Williams himself. There was such a deep restfulness about the place that it was hard to remember that only a short walk down the road Thomson first isolated the electron and Cockcroft split the atom. The colleges were empty and there was such a sweet peace and quiet in the courts and closes that it would not have surprised you to meet Erasmus on his walk in Queen's Meadow or to have come across Newton and Halley strolling in the Great Court of Trinity or, as Shaw has them in his play, anachronistically arguing with Charles II and Kneller.

"My brow is not too high, however, and I trust you will put it down to Celtic whimsey when I say I went to Emmanuel just because Swift tells us that Gulliver spent three years there. Nor, I hope, will you call me a Philistine if I tell you that after leaving Newton and Milton behind, I got just as big a thrill on Parker's Piece when I walked on the very turf where Hobbs and Hayward served their apprenticeship at the queen of games.

"Finally, I am sure you will understand why my heart leapt as I passed a certain house in St. Barnabas Road. For my mother once lived there. And, though she was only the parlourmaid, she once served tea to Rupert Brooke. I hope she had some honey for him." *

It had been a long and eventful road which led Mackay

* *News Chronicle*, January 5th, 1949.

to the mellow maturity of that Christmas at Cambridge. It was a road with many forks, and sometimes Mackay took a tentative turning which might have led to nothing more than contented obscurity. Contentment he would have achieved because the pursuit of happiness, and its frequent capture, was an absorbing passion to him. Perhaps that explains why he gave so much happiness to others, for Ian realised instinctively that the sum of happiness depends on individual contributions to the common pool. What you take depends on what you give.

So he started off his career as an industrial correspondent with a rip-roaring zest for the social side of the business. He did more than any other man to break down the barriers between Labour leaders and journalists. He became the "Ancient Mariner" of the Labour and trade union annual conferences. Woe betide you if you joined him at the end of a morning session. Your chances of lunch were small. His capacity for anecdotes and for drink was prodigious. "Un pour la rue" became a theme song with many encores. Tearing oneself away from him became a mighty and fearsome effort. You had these alternatives: you did without lunch or you skipped the afternoon session of conference. He affected a scorn for solid food, said it was effete and claimed there was more nourishment in a dram of Scotch than in a steak.

He had plenty of time for Saki's idea of an Anti-Luncheon League. He said, "In its way it is just as logical as the Anti-Liquor League. Its aim is to stop people eating as that of the prohibitionists is to stop them drinking. And I sometimes wonder if it would not have been better for the world if these two noble conceptions had been combined triumphantly in the late Victorian decades when most of our present mischiefs were growing in the smug, self-satisfied suburbs in an atmosphere of plush-framed photographs and aspidistras."

Years later he reported: "The Anti-Luncheon League was a simple little society. A small quarterly subscription entitled you to go without ninety-two luncheons. This meant that a paid-up member could go without 368 luncheons in a full year. Presumably, for they were never properly explained, the three extra meals you were allowed to go without covered leap year and enabled adventurous members to cross the international date-line without taking lunch. This happy league of abstinence seems to have been forgotten when its creator died, but a great idea of that kind is never entirely lost." *

Ian was the most persistent practitioner of Anti-Luncheon League principles that I ever met. And his first lieutenant for years was Freddie Chant, the lovable, diffidently efficient Labour Correspondent of the Press Association. Freddie's emaciated figure and pale features betrayed his membership of the Anti-Luncheon League; Ian's fine florid frame belied it. Many a time these oddly assorted companions would be deserted at the bar, and Freddy would give a fascinating little grin as Ian would bawl at the last retreating figures scuttling to the dining-room, "Traitors, traitors; may Saki's maledictions haunt you from the Shades. Same again, Frederico?"

During the T.U.C. Conference at Norwich in 1937 Ian came into his own as the great exemplar of the Anti-Luncheon League. Only a stone's throw away from St. Andrew's Hall, where the conference was held, stands a little hostelry known as the Festival House. It was generally accepted later that the Festival House took more cash in that week than in any normal year. Its genial landlord had secured a sort of extended market-day licence for the whole week. And the private back room of the inn became the headquarters of the Anti-Luncheon League, with Ian Mackay

* *News Chronicle*, September 1st, 1951

as president. He had a series of "runners" to advise him on any interesting development within the conference hall. There were moments when a shout would stop Ian in mid-sentence, and in seconds he would be in the conference hall. Then back again to the sanctum.

It was Ernie Bevin's year as conference president. Even he was inveigled into the small back room at least twice that week, although he was between bouts of breakdowns which threatened at that time to end his career. Most of the other T.U.C. chiefs were brought in, too, and some of the more socially inclined, like George Hicks, Andrew Conley, George Gibson, John Marchbanks and Robert Spence, contributed to reminiscences of the trade union movement which built up for the correspondents a background knowledge otherwise unobtainable. But shining out of the oceans of talk were the lighthouses of Ian's fabulous stories. He was a superb sprucer. There would be an element of veritable fact in all his stories. The joy came from the frills, from the fanciful embroidery which came so trippingly from his inventiveness.

In spite of Ian's preoccupation with this social development of contacts—the basis of the much-discussed items on reporters' expense sheets, discreetly obscured by the generic term "mingling"—his newspaper suffered in no way from Ian's protracted absences from the conference hall. For never is the camaraderie of the Press table demonstrated more generously than at these conferences. Besides, there was Ian's highly developed sense of selectivity. It taught him what to concentrate on, and what to discard.

There was, too, the speed with which he despatched his report once he got the opening sentence. Sometimes this gave him a bit of trouble. He would yell across the concentrated quiet of a hotel writing room, "Hey, a large Scotch for the first sentence. All I've got so far is 'Norwich, Tuesday,' and if the rest of the stuff is as accurate as that no

one can complain." Ian would blandly perambulate around
the room, looking over the shoulders of most of his intimates,
just like a defiant schoolboy ostentatiously cribbing at an
examination. Fantastic it is—in the light of his later brilliant
fertility which specialised in opening sentences of arresting
originality—to recall the hesitations of the mid- and
late-thirties.

And there was the Triumvirate.

It lasted for ten years, an arrangement quite unauthorised
and, indeed, almost defiant, although its origin was guileless.
Three of us worked as one—Ian Mackay, Hugh Chevins
and me. We comforted ourselves with the thought that our
treatment of the same story would be so distinctively
different that our respective executives would be unaware
of our collusion! And so it seemed—until some time after
the arrangement ended in 1944, when one of my chiefs
wrily remarked, "I'm glad that ring has ended. Must have
been going on for ten years, although I must say I didn't
notice it until about nineteen thirty-six!"

We were a trio with different qualities, but the differences
were outweighed by mutual interests and assessments of
men and situations. There was never a let down. We even
applied a "contracting out" clause for exclusive stories in
which our respective offices had a distinctive interest. The
arrangement ensured a sound news service, and yet gave time
for all three to relax without anxiety.

Oddly, we had only one overseas assignment as a trio
throughout the decade, although there were many occasions
when two of us were abroad together. Our solo as a trio in
foreign parts was in Brussels, where the executive of the old
Socialist International was meeting.

That is where the story of Madeleine and the frying-pan
was born. It has been retold within our circle so often, with
all the benefit of the Mackay embroidery, that it is difficult

to recall the incident in its simplicity. But, to introduce that story, let me be as discursive as Ian was.

Ian and I travelled together from London, and as we passed through Dover he enlightened me with intimate glimpses into the behind-the-scenes activities of Channel swimmers and their trainers.

Years before, it appeared, he had spent a season or two on the beach at Dover reporting the comings and goings of Channel swimmers. It must have been during parliamentary recesses, though he didn't fill in with such background because he wished to concentrate on unweaving the lurid web of commercialism and passion behind some famous cross-Channel attempts. His tales were slanderous and diverting, but he went into such detail in one case that I demanded, "How do you know all these things?" He calmly explained, "Oh, I was co-opted as a sort of adviser on newspaper publicity, and I carried the hip flask for the trainer, who banned liquor for everyone else in the camp."

Travelling to Brussels with Ian was as brief as a tube journey from Charing Cross to Trafalgar Square. Hugh Chevins came up to Brussels from Paris. Recklessly we made a pact that in our social investigation of the Belgian capital—which none of us had visited before—the rule was to be "one pub, one drink." It did not take us long to appreciate that Brussels has more pubs per head than Lancaster. In the course of the early evening we entered an *estaminet* in the secluded rue Aux Choux. It was empty, save for the florid blonde Madeleine behind the counter, polishing and beaming. Chev, appointed interpreter to the party, ordered two Amer Picons and a Pernod, to which he is faithful in those parts. As we sipped, we speculated on the sort of clientele which would patronise such an establishment.

Here was a theme which appealed to Ian's imagination. One of the main shopping avenues was barely two hundred yards away, yet this place was tucked away in a poor district of the city. We knew there was a canal nearby. Suddenly Ian spotted a trapdoor in the floor. In no time he had woven a fanciful tale.

"See those stairs at the end of the bar?" he said. "There's as elegant a suite of rooms at the top of those stairs as you'll find in Mayfair. And when the interludes are over, the drugged wines are brought in goblets of exquisite design—remember Belgium has some of the finest glass craftsmen in the world. In the brief dead watches between closing time in this exuberant city and the dawn, that trapdoor"—he pointed at it dramatically—"is lifted. Beneath that door there is a chute which leads directly to the Antwerp canal. Sometimes they don't find the bodies until they reach the docks at Antwerp. There is nothing to connect the incident with this place. You will not be surprised to learn that they do this only to well-to-do foreigners, preferably English or American whose gaucherie at love-making betrays their respectability at home, and justifies the hope that their irregularity in this place would have led them to hide their tracks here. This is the home of the perfect crime."

Ian sipped his Picon contentedly, pleased with his lightning raid into the covers of Edgar Allan Poe. And, frankly, the lights of that cheerful little *estaminet* seemed a little dimmer, the shadows more pronounced. Suddenly I clutched at Ian's sleeve, and nodded towards Madeleine. Her smiles had broadened. Her massive upper arms were hams. She increased the ferocity of her polishing. And her smile took on a new, cryptic quality. She looked like an earthy Mona Lisa. I hissed my protest, "Ianto, you damn fool, she understood you." He was a bland one. He murmured, "We'll soon see. Break our rule and have a second drink here and get her to join us. She'll welcome the extra custom. Chevinski, ask her over."

27

She came with alacrity. She was soon babbling away the main items of her pathetic little life story. She had been respectably married for years until her husband had been killed by a faulty crane while loading a canal barge. There was a triumphant gleam in Ian's eyes as Chev translated this bit. Then she became a little coy, hinting with elephantine delicacy that although another term of matrimony was her objective she was content at the moment to go on with her selective experiments among her wide circle of male acquaintances. She lowered her eyes more from contentment than modesty, as Chev gave his enthusiastic translation.

Then Ian noticed her profile. Her nose was so flat that its point was in a straight line with her forehead and chin. And it was then that Ian put his immortal question. He demanded, "Chev, ask her who slapped her across the face with the back of a frying-pan."

Madeleine looked quickly from Ian to Chev for the interpretation. A remarkable thing happened. Chev, usually so fluent and self-possessed, blushed and stammered. His delicacy had him tongue-tied. "What's holding you up?" demanded Ian roguishly. Chev lied gallantly. He said, "I can't for the life of me remember the French for frying-pan."

Ian turned to Madeleine, and, in passably good French, explained that he was fascinated by the straightness of her profile. He added that his interest was possibly due to its contrast with his own craggy, rugged features and noble beak. Madeleine quickly volunteered, "It was a weakness in my childhood, monsieur, for pressing my nose against window panes. Alas, my family tried in vain to cure me." She shrugged her ample shoulders resignedly. "Then, it was not a frying-pan, madame?" Ian begged, with much relief. Madeleine trilled delightedly. For a moment she recaptured what must have been the beauty of her girlhood. After she had wiped the tears from her eyes, she gravely assured Ian,

Tais-toi! C'est Monsieur Mackay
qui parle!!

Scribe Bar. 1946

Lancaster

—by Osbert Lancaster.

29

"No, monsieur, it was *not* a frying-pan." Whereupon, Ian turned to Chev and with equal solemnity repeated, "Monsieur, it was *not* a frying-pan, and now having relieved our anxiety I think we might with propriety beg madame's permission to depart."

Madeleine assured Ian she found him enchanting, if droll, and begged him to return. There were, however, too many other distractions in Brussels. It was a happy week, made carefree by the co-operation of such British Labour and trade union leaders as James Walker, the steelmen's leader whose rugged heartiness was unimpeded by his blindness, and Willie Gillies, the Labour Party's International Secretary, whose natural caution was temporarily submerged by his anxiety to convey the British point of view in the strained talks then going on.

There were no professional surprises at this conference as there were to be a few years later when Ian and I went to Düsseldorf to cover the talks between leaders of the Federation of British Industries and their opposite numbers on the Reichsgruppe Industrie. The significance of that trip, it turned out, depended largely on what had happened in England before we crossed to Germany.

It was then the custom of the Ministry of Labour to conduct the industrial correspondents around one region after another for an investigation into work being done. This was primarily the idea of Sam Chaloner, the Ministry's Press Officer, who had the quaint notion that both the newspapers and his Ministry would benefit from a properly organised probe into the problems of the day. I say quaint because he was the only Government Press Officer of his time who did anything like this. On this occasion we were touring parts of the West Country and the southern counties. At the main centres we met Ministry officials and the leading industrialists and trade union chiefs of the area.

The talks were frank, and no questions were barred.
One morning in Gloucester we were discussing labour
supply problems when an official let slip the name of
Corsham. It was an unfamiliar name. Thousands of
labourers were wanted, it seemed, for Corsham. Finding
them was not a problem, but housing them was. Some of
them were lodged in Bristol and others in Bath. I asked
where and what Corsham was. There was then a hurried
consultation among the top Ministry men, who asked us to
forget that we had ever heard the name of Corsham. They
explained in confidence that the Corsham project was a
mighty series of subterranean storage depots and repair bases
for military and aeronautical equipment. It was highly
secret. Its name should not have been disclosed. Please
would we forget about it?

There was plenty of encouragement to forgetfulness in the
departure and journey to Düsseldorf. We were seen off by
Vivian Brodzky and his wife Paula, as emotional as they are
big-hearted. Paula looked up at our compartment, the tears
streaming down her cheeks. We were leaving for a country
where she would not be welcome because of her religion.
She clutched a wispy handkerchief and sobbed, "Don't let
them do anything to you, you darling boys." That gave Ian
his theme for our journey to Harwich—and how he
developed it! It brought home to us the business we were on.
It seemed a rum affair, in March 1938, for the leaders of the
F.B.I., spokesmen of big business in Britain, to be going to
Germany for an amiable agreement with industrial leaders
who must include men connected with frenzied Nazi
rearmament. It all looked very dubious. Ian summed up by
remarking, "Fancy shaking hands with a bunch of bastards
who wouldn't let Paula in!"

Brandy, said Ian at Harwich, was the obvious preparation
for the night-crossing. We were the last in the saloon and as

the Dutch bar-tender looked tired Ian suggested we should take a half-bottle along to our two-berth cabin just in case. He was in the upper berth. He was furious when the lurching ship sent our suitcases sliding across the floor of the cabin, first towards the scuppers and then back below my berth. The noise the slithering made interrupted his sonorous recital from a translation of Horace's Odes, which was then his bedtime reading. He had just been talking about people who achieve immortality merely through being contented. Philip the Patrician was returning from the wars when he noticed a man lolling in the shade of a barber's shop, paring his nails and whistling. Philip was impressed by such contentment and sent his slave to ask him whom he was and what he did.

"Listen to this!" Ian commanded. The boat lurched. Our suitcases were coming back to us. "Ignore that," he called crossly. Then he intoned,

> "Menas is his name,
> Of moderate fortune, but of honest fame;
> A public crier, who a thousand ways
> Bustles to get, and then enjoys his ease.
> A boon companion 'mongst his equals known,
> And the small house he lives in is his own."

Our suitcases were leaving us again for the scuppers. Ian ignored them. His voice was full of excitement. "Listen to that last line again, 'And the small house he lives in is his own.' What does the whole of that passage suggest to you?" Yawning, I shouted back, "One of three things. Philip was a patient bloke to wait for all that information. Menas was a talkative and garrulous old sot to disclose so much to a stranger, or the slave was a hell of a good and fast reporter."

Our suitcases were coming back to us. Ian could hardly wait for them to arrive before yelling above the din, "Yes, yes, I grant all that, but just imagine, Menas owned his house. What the hell did they pay their public criers in those days? Do you suppose they had a building society in Rome? I must look that up. There may be a record somewhere of the interest they charged."

The suitcases were leaving us again. There was enough of a pause for Ian's thoughts to take a new turn. "Damn it," he yelled, "what a hell of a good name for a columnist—Menas. Menas, the contented town crier. It's short and it's significant. Boy, that's a good one to remember." Back the suitcases were coming. There was a yelp from above. "Pass me that bloody brandy, quickly." A few hours later the steward bringing us tea graciously apologised, on behalf of the Dutch shipowners, for the dirtiest crossing of the winter.

The Nazi customs officials stopped badgering us just in time to avoid an incident, after they boarded the train on the Dutch-German border. They were punctilious rather than arrogant. But the sight of the swastika badges on their uniforms distressed Ian. He was getting more and more truculent in his replies. His fists were clenching involuntarily. Just about two more questions and he would have exploded.

We were in the lounge of the Park Hotel in Düsseldorf, where the F.B.I. conference was taking place, before calmness returned to him. And then, characteristically, he made a discovery which gave him a kick. Franzie, the bartender, was an old acquaintance who had worked for years in many London hotels. And, as we sauntered into the cocktail bar Ian gave Franzie a joyful greeting, "Franzie, you black-hearted old bastard, what the hell do you mean by forsaking us for this dump?" As they were pump-handling each other, I glanced hastily around the bar. For when Ian gave a joyful greeting the world heard it. There were two stylishly dressed women on high stools at the counter, and over at a small table near the window was a depressing little man, in rusty black, with a bald head, gazing short-sightedly

c

through pince-nez at a newspaper. The women glanced curiously at this noisy intruder and then resumed their chatting. The little man was still intent on his newspaper.

Then I was introduced to Franzie, a good-looking, sturdily built man of about thirty. Good natured, too. He murmured, "I can see you are still the same old Mr. Mackie, but I ought to tell you there are some people around here without your sense of humour." And then Ian's eye saw the tiny swastika badge in the lapel of Franzie's smart, white jacket. I saw it at the same moment. I closed my eyes and waited for the outburst from Ian. "This is it," I thought. But when I opened my eyes, Ian ordered two drinks in the coldest, most impersonal voice I ever heard him use. And with equally impersonal punctilio, Franzie served them. He understood.

In came Sir William Larke and his colleagues from the Federation of British Industries and their German hosts. I introduced Ian to Sir William, who, in turn, presented us to the general who led the German team. He looked a thinner, younger Hindenberg, but he was courteous—and intrigued by our presence. The general beckoned a smartly dressed ramrod of a man to join us. This was a colonel and almost a caricature of a Junker, with the sabre mark on his cheek and his monocle. He spoke English, with clipped precision, and this was the climax of his talk with Ian and myself:

"From where have you come?"

"London; we crossed last night."

"Yes, yes, but you don't spend all your time in London, do you? Don't you travel around?"

"Oh, yes. As a matter of fact, we broke off a tour to come on this trip."

"That's interesting. Where did you go?"

"Oh, around the West Country, Bristol, Gloucester, and then down to Portsmouth."

"And Corsham?"

"Corsham? Where's that?"

"Come, come, gentlemen. You should know your country much better. Corsham is much more interesting than the places you mention. Newer, too."

We telephoned our stories on the talks to London before sauntering out to a bench in a park to talk about the shock we had received.

Four days later we took a taxi from Liverpool Street Station to Whitehall, where we reported our talk with the colonel. Whitehall was as startled as we had been. Three years later, the day after the heart of Swansea had been torn out by the Luftwaffe, Ernest Bevin told Ian and myself in a train going down to Swansea how he had chuckled when he had come across the dossier containing a report of this incident. "Chuckled?" Ian queried. "Yes," Ernest explained, convulsed again at the recollection, "because written in the margin was, 'For journalists these two seem reputable and reliable.' What do you think of that as a testimonial?"

We guessed the author of this sardonic comment. Ernest nodded confirmation. He was not particularly fond of Humbert Wolfe, either. Wolfe, a brilliant litterateur and distinguished civil servant, was reputed to be the author of a slanderous, though amusing, jibe at the probity of British journalists.

"You cannot hope
   to bribe, or twist,
thank God! the
   British journalist.
But seeing what
   the man will do
unbribed, there's
   no occasion to."

Wolfe could not resist a wisecrack.

Yet Ian did not place his hectic German visit at the top of his list of memorable assignments as an industrial correspondent. That position of honour was occupied by the visit of King Edward VIII to the mining valleys of South Wales. And all because of a single spoken phrase.

That visit of Edward VIII was a two-day tour, starting from a sleepy railway siding in the pleasant Vale of Glamorgan, where the King alighted to be greeted by the two Ministers in attendance, Sir Kingsley Wood, Minister of Health, and Mr. Ernest Brown, Minister of Labour—and about twenty of us correspondents. The tour was through part of the lower Rhondda, up to Merthyr, down through the Aberdare Valley, and over next day to some of the western valleys of Monmouthshire—all of them areas where the hideous poverty of a decade had left a listless, disillusioned people. And here was the Prince coming to see them. For it was as Prince of Wales that the King was still known. It was fantastic, hysterical, emotional—sometimes frightening. For the King was moved—and the people swept police barriers aside in their eagerness to demonstrate their appreciation of his presence.

In the ruins of the great Cyfarthfa steelworks, in Merthyr, the King turned a corner, and there he saw a great retort, which had toppled on its side and was now rusted, with ivy clinging to its sides. At that moment it was a grandstand for a group of white-faced, pathetically clad men who had once worked in this famous plant. The King blanched. He took one step back, and murmured in a horrified whisper to Ernest Brown, "It can't be true."

The King found that this and many other things like it were too tragically true. He was so shaken by the end of the first day that, in the drill hall at Mountain Ash, where he was supposed merely to look at some handicrafts which the long-workless miners and their wives had made to cheat despair, he decided impulsively to speak.

It was a short speech—a simple, sincere tribute to the gallantry of a people who had clung heroically to their self-respect. And in the middle of a sentence more words failed to come. There was a lump in the royal throat. The King took out his handkerchief. Then he waved his arm disconsolately, and turned to leave the hall. There was a grim, throat-clutching silence until two middle-aged women near the door started to sing, "Among our ancient mountains . . . ," the first four words of "God Bless the Prince of Wales." Then the people became a mighty choir. They hadn't needed a rehearsal. Their conductor's baton was the beat of their hearts.

There were many times during those two days when the correspondents' cars, from the third to the fifteenth in that shining crocodile, were jammed by the multitude. In the square at Aberdare I was travelling with Ian and Hannen Swaffer when thirty to forty men, women and youngsters jumped on the running boards, the bonnet and the roof, and we were trapped inside. Swaffer was saying that even if we were crushed and killed it would be a small gesture of atonement from the outer world to these victims of public neglect and indifference. And from the other window Ian Mackay was peering out over the shoulders or between the elbows of our guests to try to classify which of the Aberdarians were Brythons, Celts or Goidels, the three tributaries to the Cymric race. He kept shouting to me, "Now that girl with a shawl over her head, the dark one with the high cheek-bones, is she a Goidel or a Brython?"

In Merthyr, where people elbowed each other to scrutinise us through the windows, one woman annoyed both Hannen Swaffer and Ian Mackay by shouting, "Come here, Olwen, there are two men in here with long hair, one grey and the other black; come and see if they are father and son." This was a particularly distressing remark for Swaff, who only ten seconds before had murmured, "There's always a crowd like this when I come to Merthyr—you should have seen the way I was mobbed when I came to speak here last winter." But Swaff was as good as Ian Mackay in verbal extrication. In the embarrassed silence which followed the invitation to Olwen, Swaff observed acidly, "Obviously that woman is not a native of Merthyr. Come in from one of the outlying villages, I expect."

It was Swaffer, too, who was the author of the most quoted remark from our camp in that tour. We came to a place where the King had entered an ex-servicemen's hut, used as a communal workshop. The police threw a close cordon across the path leading to the hut—for the King was in danger of suffocation, or of being crushed by those who had already entered the hut with him. And our car-load was on the wrong side of the cordon. We pleaded with the police inspector to let us through. He glanced over his shoulder at the hut behind him. He was horrified. Its sides appeared to be bulging. He shook his head. Swaffer turned to the intrigued crowd, threw his arms wide open and his distinctive head well back, to yell dramatically to the mountain tops on the other side of the valley, "They won't let me in. They won't let me in." He looked and sounded like a prophet shut out of Paradise. The crowd was fascinated —but silent. Ian sauntered over to Swaff, and tugged his sleeve. He said, "There's only one thing for it, Swaff. You'll have to start a rival show. Get the crowd—and the King—to come to you." Swaff pondered for a moment, then grinned. For once, the Dean of Fleet Street had no reply.

It was not until we were streaking down the dark, silent valley of the Taff towards Cardiff at the end of the day that we fully realised the disadvantages of trying to report events which many of us had not seen, or conversations we had not heard. Some sayings of the King we had heard second, third, and even fourth hand. One such phrase, in particular, struck us as most significant. Someone had reported that the King, shaking hands with a long-unemployed man at the top of the Valley, had said, "Something should be done." In the next car they were saying the King had said, "Something ought to be done." And in the car behind that, "Something must be done."

There was some heavy pondering and discussion in every car in the procession, down through Treforest, under the shadow of Norman Castell Coch, and right into the suburbs of Cardiff. The philological and political experts were having a field night. There was a mighty difference—far more than the odd word—between the phrases as variously reported. And everyone realised that out of all the incidents and out of all the thousands of words exchanged that day this one phrase would be the keynote of all newspaper reports. There had to be unanimity. But how? Time was getting short. Indeed, by the time we reached our hotel in Cardiff there would be barely twenty minutes left before the stampede to the telephones.

Fortunately, most of us were staying at the Angel Hotel. There had to be a conference. I was to sleep on a "shakedown" bed in the corner of one of the hotel lounges that night. Therefore, my room was most suitable, because it was the most commodious, for a Press conference. Everyone turned up. It was a short but sharp meeting. There were supporters for each phrase. It was Ian Mackay who suddenly ended the argument by demanding, "Who actually heard the King use these words?" There were two—the respected ascetic Vaughan Davies, who was representing *The Times*, and an agency man. They agreed that the King had said, "Something *must* be done." That settled it. "Must" was very much the desired word.

But after our stories had been sent, the argument started again. Supposing, just supposing, that the King had not used that phrase, and that he had been misheard—the political consequences might be serious, for his critics would accuse him of interfering in politics and of embarrassing Baldwin's Government at a time when the Opposition was bitterly critical of the Government's employment policy. Ian dramatised our misgivings in the early hours of the morning. "Supposing," he declared, "that on the very day this monarch has won our affection for his humanity and sympathy to the highest degree ever, we should have contributed to his abdication." We laughed, and accused Ian of exaggeration and heroics. He was unusually grave, and refused to dissolve his mood to our badinage: but the King abdicated within a month.

Ian's appreciation of the significance of the King's remark got heavy reinforcement the next afternoon. We joined Ernest Brown, a most approachable Minister of Labour, on the platform of Newport Station while waiting for the London train. We had heard that the King had been outspoken in his condemnation of the effects of mass unemployment on a community. Further, we knew that Mrs. Simpson had travelled to Monmouthshire to dine with the King in the royal coach the previous evening.

Although Mrs. Simpson had been granted her decree *nisi* two or three weeks earlier, the British Press still remained silent on their meetings. The storm clouds were in the air. Ian and I questioned Ernest Brown on his impressions of the tour. He looked gloomy, and kept plucking his underlip. In his *basso profundo* voice he intoned, "Very disturbing, involving questions of the highest constitutional importance. Sir Kingsley Wood and I regard it as our duty to make a formal report to the Cabinet. You must excuse me from indicating the nature of our report." That gave Ian his theme for the train journey to London. He could not resist speculating, "Do you think the King, knowing there is a crisis coming, deliberately overstepped the bounds of constitutional propriety to show his real interests and to rally support if he needs it?"

I replied tersely, "No." I am a man of peace, and I like dozing in trains.

"Why?" demanded Ian. "Because," I retorted, "he wouldn't have chosen that moment to say what he did. He would have seen that more of us would have been around."

Ian thought for a moment. "Perhaps," he insisted, "that was a piece of royal subtlety. Besides, it might have been a compliment to our grape-vine." He was reluctant to let go his hunch that we had kicked a pebble which would start an avalanche of history.

Not that he was always so intense. This, indeed, was the period—and it went on right up to the start of the war—when he created his reputation for being "a broth of a bhoy," and "the last of the Bohemians." He evolved what he regarded as a pleasant routine. It saw him right for half the year, he explained, and gave him time to prepare his diversions for the other half.

It was an impressive arrangement. He would set off from his office in Bouverie Street on Maundy Thursday to cover the Easter conferences, and then hop from resort to resort, from one conference to another, right through to October, when the annual conference of the Labour Party ended what he called his programme of "pounding the promenades" of this country. His calendar was a peculiarly professional affair. To him Easter weekend was Co-operative Party weekend, there were civil servants' weeks in May, engineers' and railwaymen's weeks in June, a miners' week in

July, a Confederation week in August, and the T.U.C. week in September.

Sometimes he would pretend to complain if two unions held their conferences in the same week. He would protest, "I can't be in two places at once." And then he would take odd weeks of his own holidays at the strangest times, like the first week in December, in the most unexpected places, like a cottage in Derbyshire.

And all the time he would joke that he was always being "done" because he alleged he never took the full holidays to which he was entitled by agreement, and that, in fact, by 1938 he was working off what should have been his third week's holiday in 1936. He lived in a jolly, madcap world of restless enjoyment, of which his work was part. And he did outrageous things, like throwing his dentures over the pier at Weston-super-Mare because they did not fit properly. This led to one of his most celebrated party tricks: spearing a pickle-onion with his sole remaining tooth.

And in wintertime, when he came back to London because there were no conferences to attend, he would hold us up at night from hareing off to our more conventional homes, just as he had held up union leaders and delegates throughout the summer from eating in the middle of the day because of his loyalty to the Anti-Luncheon League. At that time he was living in scanty comfort in a flat in a Fleet Street court, which he always referred to as "The Drain." He would explain, "Shows how conscientious I am. I live and sleep on top of my job." And when we ultimately caught our trains, Ian, having tossed well-embroidered maledictions after us for being suburbanites—"and, strike me, you'll be parading in rolled umbrellas next"—would wait for the sub-editors on the morning papers to join him in midnight sessions.

He was ever welcome, for his quick, perceptive mind, his

prodigious memory, and his fabulous, fanciful tales. He told all of them with impressive conviction, though some of them were far-fetched.

One of his favourites concerned a nebulous old friend of his called Glendower. Glendower had some sort of job connected with Parliament. When Parliament was sitting Glendower was its eminently respectable, assiduous servant. He was a bachelor who lodged in Brixton. He lived frugally and saved most of his salary. When Parliament rose for the long summer recess Glendower would hurry off to his brother, a rector in Wales, bearing gifts for his brother and sister-in-law and for each of their many children. He was a welcome guest, and a devout one, too. He was a model worshipper at every service on that first weekend after the rising of Parliament. But on the following Tuesday Glendower would dash back to London; the next morning he would leave for Paris on the Golden Arrow. That night there would be a happy reconciliation in a discreet apartment "quite near the rue Royale," kept by a Madame Marthe. Glendower was "home" again.

And for the whole of the parliamentary recess, Glendower became the complete boulevardier, resting or reading the French classics by day, sallying forth for an apéritif in the evening, settling down for a concentrated appreciation of Parisian night-life before returning to the solicitous Madame Marthe in the early hours of the morning. He was known to all Madame Marthe's friends and relatives, Ian would tell you, as an English milord, and "he comported himself as such."

On the Friday before Parliament resumed, Glendower would return to Wales, bringing many souvenirs and mementoes for his brother's family, and again behaving with commendable circumspection as befitted the rector's brother. Then he would return to the equally commendable execution of his duties. Ian would sigh, "What a wonderful routine. Everybody happy—no harm done to anyone." "But what about the hypocrisy?" Ian was once challenged. He replied, "Most of life is hypocrisy."

That story may or may not have been true. Ian, from the polishing of its recital, came, if not to believe it, to regard it as an admirable pattern for living. All the same, Ian had few complaints about his own style of living in those days. He was contented because he compounded at will the pleasures of companionship with the relaxation of solitude. His front door was exactly ninety-seven steps from Fleet Street. And his bed-sitting room was a library. He retired and rose when he pleased. He had no one else to consider. No ties. No obligations.

Yet once, and only once in my experience, he envied us, whose ways were more formal. It was on a night that newspaper offices closed down for Christmas. Most of us were heavily laden. In those days money was the only limitation to buying. There we were, standing around the bar with so many parcels to carry home that some of us had little lists clutched in our hands to make certain that we would forget none of our gifts. Time came for "loading up." I handed Ian my list, and said, "Check these, old boy." He pleaded, "What's the hurry? Just have one for the road."

He turned to me, and muttered in an unfamiliar tone, "You lucky blighter, having a home and kids to go to, giving and receiving presents, guzzling yourselves stupid. You don't know how lucky you are."

I was astounded. Here was the man who for years had taunted us for settling down. I was abashed, too, for my thoughtlessness in forgetting that he would be alone. So I pressed him to come home with me, or to join us on the morrow for Christmas. "Not on your life," he replied, "because Christmas is a family affair and I'm no family man.

My altruistic pleasure in seeing others happy over Christmas does not stop me longing to see it over." I chaffed, "Don't tell me you, of all people, are an unreformed Scrooge?" Ian replied, "No, as I've said, I'm all for you others letting your hair down, but mine's the sort of life where Christmas finds the chink."

And that moment in marched a woman we called Gabe, a fairly well-known and prosperous feature writer at that time. She had a good sense of feminine style, and her artifice helped to hide the ravages of a series of broken marriages. She never talked about her troubles, and was accepted around Fleet Street as a good sort. She joined us, and Ian asked her what she was doing for Christmas. Cryptically she replied, "Going in search of it. I've got my car outside." She said casually a few minutes later, "Can I give you a lift?" He agreed, and off they went. Gabe drove Ian down to her sister in Oxfordshire, a woman prominent in local public life. It turned out to be one of the happiest Christmases Ian had spent. His hostess took him to a local children's hospital and he was a last-minute stand-in for Father Christmas—a role he was to fulfil regularly, years later, at the mammoth children's parties given by the patrons of the Fitzroy Tavern in Bloomsbury.

Ian, though, was coming dangerously near to drifting before the war. He lacked an anchorage. He was competent and well informed, but there was only the occasional sparkle of the brilliance which later dazzled the newspaper world.

Then a tiny incident had major consequences for Ian Mackay. One of the most highly respected industrial writers at that time was John Vernon Ratcliffe, of *The Times*, a man of impeccable probity and exquisite manners. And, it turned out, a man of acute perception. He mentioned to a few of us one day, "There is one man among us who might be a genius if he only had a compass." When he mentioned

Ian Mackay, we looked at him in some surprise, mainly because many of Ian's characteristics were abhorred by the abstemious and correct John Ratcliffe. We found a way of passing Ratcliffe's remark on to Ian without embarrassment. Ian shrugged his shoulders, and gave a calculated impression of cursory interest. It soon became obvious, however, that Ian valued and appreciated the good opinion of the fastidious Ratcliffe. He showed his reaction by increased assiduity not only to his job but to the creation of the formal Industrial Correspondents' Group, of which he became chairman in succession to Ratcliffe.

Ian was chairman when we made one of our first formal tours of the war. Dr. Leslie Burgin, a friendly but not self-confident parliamentarian, had been made Minister of Supply. The Government and people of Ulster, where there was still abnormal unemployment and unused productive capacity, were eager to make their fullest contribution to Britain's defence. On grounds of loyalty, availability of men and machines, and comparative immunity from air raids they were demanding war contracts. So they invited Dr. Burgin over to Belfast to see for himself what they had to offer, and they invited the industrial correspondents over to tell the people of England how eager Ulster was to play its part in the war.

One of our party was Ben Francis, of the Communist *Daily Worker*. The Communists had decided by this time that the war was an unholy crusade and should be opposed in every way. Ian and I were introduced to some officials as soon as we came off the gangway at Larne. Casually, one of these officials asked us to point out Ben Francis. It was no trouble at all, for Ben was standing only a yard or so away. We called over to him but he merely waved to us, as he was chatting to someone. Ian said to the official, "We'll bring him over in a moment to introduce him to you." There was

— THE ORIGINAL MACKOLUMNIST

—by Strube.

a flicker of embarrassment over the official's features. He replied hastily, "I don't want to trouble you. You see, I'm the officer in charge of secutiry here, and I have been instructed to keep Mr. Francis under observation from the moment he lands until he goes back over the water." Ian and I offered to pledge Ben's good conduct. The officer declined stiffly.

We were a little perplexed. It was the period of the "phoney war." Our appreciation of security was in its infancy. We had known and liked Ben Francis for years. Should we warn him that he was under observation? I suggested we should tell him that we were all under an obligation as guests of the Northern Ireland Government to confine our activities strictly to our jobs. It would, I argued, be doing Ben a good turn without doing our hosts a disservice. Ian agreed, but when he mentioned this to Ben we had a surprise. Ben, with his twinkling eyes and ready laugh, replied, "Oh, I know. They're on the watch here. Very keen. You know that bloke you were talking to on the quay at Larne? He's one of the security bosses around here."

In our team too was the Marquess of Donegall. He was there as a columnist for the *Sunday Dispatch*. He is an amiable companion, a good mixer, with no side about him. Like the rest of us he agreed that on the few occasions when a formal reply was needed on behalf of the Press, our spokesman should be Ian. That was all right until we got to Belfast. And then the change came rapidly. We met an official of the reception committee who asked that introductions should be made. Ian presented us. As he went down the line, he murmured perfunctorily, "Donegall." The official stopped as if pole-axed. "I beg your pardon," he stammered, "did I hear aright?" Ian repeated, "Donegall. He's a columnist." The official swallowed hard and gasped, "The Marquess of Donegall?" Donegall nodded. "Oh, but sir, there's obviously been a grave error." He darted away, and brought back a Minister, who insisted on Donegall joining the official party.

In fairness to Donegall, I must say he went reluctantly. For the rest of the visit we saw him only from a distance. He sat at the top table on all occasions, and there were times when the Ulstermen were tempted to make more fuss of the Marquess than of Burgin, upon whom so much depended for Ulster. Ian mumbled, "What with a Communist in the dog-house, and a columnist up among the stars, how the hell do they expect us to keep a team together?"

He recalled a similar experience to the whisking away of Donegall. One of our closest friends before the war had been Lord Kinnoull, who had joined the Labour Party. He was frequently down at Transport House. He was a charming, modest companion—at times too modest. We used to say to him, "Harley, why don't you assert yourself a bit more and get a job worthy of your talents?" And dear Kinnoull used to murmur, "That's the trouble, I've so few talents."

One day Ian bumped into him in Edinburgh. "Where are you going Harley?" he cried. Kinnoull explained he was going on to Perth to see a solicitor. "I'm going up that way, so I'll join you, if I may," Ian suggested. Kinnoull was delighted, and off they went to Perth.

"You should have seen what happened," Ian recalled delightedly. "They'd put poor old Harley up near the servants' quarters, next to me, but when they discovered who he was there was the manager and all the flunkies in the hotel practically carrying poor old Harley and his little weekend case out of his box-room to install him in the royal suite.

"They rooted out the Provost, the Lord Lieutenant of the county, and the lairds for fifty miles around to do him honour. It turns out he's practically a king around there. I caught a glimpse of him about two days later. He broke away for a moment to have a word with me. It was four days later before we could have a noggin together—and that was back in Edinburgh, where he was just another citizen like me. You've got to be careful where you take your titled pals."

The Donegall incident was not the end of our complications in Belfast. On the second or third day of the tour we were to be the guests at luncheon of some distinguished citizens at the exclusive Union Club. It was a massive affair. All Belfast was there. But in the cloakroom crush someone said, "They've not invited George Thomas, because he's on the *Daily Herald*. This is a very exclusive Tory club, and there's a rule or tradition which bans a Socialist from crossing the portals."

We promptly decided that such discrimination against our old colleague George was an outrage. If George couldn't eat, neither would we. I said to Ian, "You are the gaffer, find out what's happening." Ian asked a flustered official, who retorted, "Everyone who has been invited is here. We can make no alterations now. It's too late." Ian reported back to us. We looked around the vast and crowded dining-room. We decided to walk out in protest—back to our hotel a few yards away. Ian was quite pleased. He still belonged to the Anti-Luncheon League. He took us to the bar to "hold a conference." I asked, "Where's George, by the way?" We inquired of the hall porter. He said he had seen Mr. Thomas walking out about half an hour earlier. We sighed, "Poor old George, he's so embarrassed that he's gone for a walk."

Two hours later, George Thomas strolled in. "Where have you been,?" we all demanded. George looked at us in surprise. He said, "In the luncheon at the Union Club, of course. Where do you think?" We demanded, "Where were you sitting?" He replied, "Oh, behind a pillar at the far end of the room but I could hear perfectly. Very good lunch, didn't you think?" He was the only one of us who had eaten. Ian led a deputation around to our hosts to apologise. They were most gracious about it. We did our best to see that Ulster got a good show. And we solemnly agreed that rumours are dangerous.

Many people, even colleagues in Fleet Street, used to sympathise with us for having to attend so many conferences. They thought Ian quite abnormal for his zest for such "talking shops." Some conferences can be boring. Others can be embarrassing, when controlled by officials with a sense of inspired news-value. They know better than the Press table what should be published in the newspapers. Their own speeches, for instance. But there are many fundamentally important, even dramatic, conferences.

Ian had a theory that the best stories from even the best conferences rarely get into the newspapers. There are always valued friendships to be protected, there are space limitations, there is the law of libel.

"But if, which God forbid, I ever write my memoirs," Ian would muse (he did, in whimsical fragments among the million words of his postwar columns and essays), "I will have to find a way of describing what happened behind the scenes immediately after Ernie Bevin lacerated George Lansbury in public at Brighton, what went on after Stafford Cripps, George Strauss and Nye Bevan were expelled from the Labour Party at Southport, and how Churchill dominated the Labour Party Conference at Bournemouth."

That last was the most dramatic of all. It was the conference which approved the entry of Labour leaders into Churchill's wartime Government. We wore our summer clothes that Whitsun, summer clothes most of us had bought before the war. France was falling and there was M. Léon Blum among us, forcing tears from those who understood barely one word of what he was saying long before Philip Noel-Baker recited his masterly translation.

But the most human story happened nightly at nine o'clock in the lounge of the cliff-top hotel which was the Party executive headquarters. That was the hour of the B.B.C. news—expected at any time to announce the Government changes, the elevation to high office of men among us. Five minutes before nine o'clock the lounge would be deserted. Little groups would then rise from the benches on the lawn outside, stretch themselves in the balmy air, and saunter with studied nonchalance towards the hotel. More sophisticated types in the subterranean "snug" or in the spacious saloon presided over by Rita, the pin-up girl of the conference, would ostentatiously glance at their wrist-watches and "knock them back." Others would emerge on the stairs, with letters in their hands as if making for the post-box. And the hall porter would switch on the radio loudspeaker in the corner of the packed lounge at precisely fifteen seconds to nine.

When the announcer came to the words, "Further additions to the Government have been announced from number ten Downing Street. They are . . ." the suspense was excruciating. Most of the leaders in that lounge had their wives or families with them, usually on the arms of their chairs. Some of them had kept their secrets well, for when their names were announced their children gasped delightedly, "Oh, Daddy!" only to be hushed sternly by those who wanted to hear the rest of the bulletin. It would not be too cynical to suppose that some may have hoped to hear their own names, but generally there was little evidence of self-interest.

One leader's name was not mentioned—to our intense surprise—until we were packing up to go home. And then, as the taxis were queueing up to take us to the railway station,

he stalked into the telephone box beside the front door. The
door of the kiosk did not shut properly. "Is that the Ministry
of . . .? This is your new Minister speaking. I will be at
Waterloo at seven o'clock, and will you please arrange to
have me met?" Yet I doubt whether this was the conference
incident Ian would have picked out as most memorable,
although he was standing beside me when it happened.

The moral of that week to Ian was Rita. She was a
handsome gal. Her efficiency was impressive even to us
with long experience of such service. It became our custom
to congratulate in Rita's bar those of our new Ministers
who were socially inclined, and equally our custom to
inform Rita of the status of her new customer. Rita would
incline her head with dignity, and murmur briskly,
"Congratulations. What will you have, sir?" and then
proceed to serve the order. No fuss, no fluster, and an equal
eagerness to respond to the clamorous demands of less
exalted customers.

Ian would rhapsodise, "See what I mean? That's the
spirit of England, get on with the job whatever you are
doing. This is no time for flagwagging or of goggling at our
new rulers. Brisk efficiency is what's needed." And he would
gaze admiringly at her as an example of the workers of
England. Henry Philpott of the *Daily Herald* declared, "I
must say, Ian, that your taste in the selection of a specimen
for your moralising does you credit." And Ian would
confess, "Watching her gives me no pain."

The mighty events of that week were to affect the industrial
correspondents as intimately as the rest of our fellow-
countrymen for the remainder of the war. For Labour
leaders were appointed to most of the departments with
which we were most closely associated. Ernest Bevin was at
the Ministry of Labour and National Service, Herbert
Morrison at the Ministry of Supply—before Lord

Beaverbrook went there—Hugh Dalton at the Ministry of Economic Warfare and later at the Board of Trade, and David Grenfell at the Mines Department.

And of all these, indeed of all Ministers, it was Ernest Bevin with whom we worked most closely and most constructively. The orders and regulations which flowed from his Ministry for the mobilisation of Britain's manpower compelled us to become authorities in the interpretation of "Whitehallese," and Bevin did his utmost to make our task easier.

His affability in the early days of his Ministry was all the more remarkable because he had declared war on the Press in general and industrial correspondents in particular as late as 1937, when the London bus strike had paralysed the capital for six weeks. The trouble then was Bevin's conviction that we were too "hand in glove" with the strike leaders, the lively Frank Snelling, Bert Papworth and Bill Jones. We had to produce a story every day during that strike. Bevin was prepared to talk to us only about twice, rarely thrice, a week, and sometimes what he had to tell us was hardly worth publishing. His Transport and General Workers' Union had, and has, no established Press or public relations officer. You talked to Bevin or no one, and Bevin was usually unavailable. Snelling, Papworth and Jones, on the other hand, were always on hand. Their command of the strikers was complete. Their sense of publicity highly developed. So Bevin was annoyed.

One day he called a Press conference at the foot of the stairs in Transport House. He came down the stairs towards us, ponderously, with his face clouded in anger. He stood on the bottom step. He announced, "I will read you this statement on one condition only—that you publish it as I have written it, commas and all." There was a murmur of protest. We could not commit our newspapers without knowing what was in the statement. And we tried to explain our dilemma to Bevin. He seemed not to have heard us. He waited for us to finish, and then repeated inflexibly, "Commas and all." Whereupon a lanky Australian, who happened to be acting as a substitute that day for a regular industrial correspondent, drawled rudely, "How do we know you know where to put the commas?" We were more shocked than Bevin at this insolence, and we told the Australian what we thought. Bevin read his short statement, turned on his heel and climbed the stairs to his office. His statement was accurately and adequately summarised in all newspapers the next morning.

But Bevin had been on the defensive for three years. And now in 1940, he had become the virtual arbiter of the destinies of all adults in the land. We were dubious about our relations with him. But it was Bevin himself who put us at our ease.

Almost from the moment he walked into old Montagu House, in Whitehall, then the headquarters of the Ministry of Labour, he proved that the past had buried itself. We were privy to some of the innermost secrets of the Ministry, even to the consternation Bevin had created within a day of taking office when he threw down a piece of paper and declared, "Here are my plans for the full mobilisation of civilians." The only other Minister who regarded even the most exalted civil servants as his instruments to this extent was Lord Beaverbrook, down the road at Millbank, at the Ministry of Aircraft Production.

Bevin even permitted Ian Mackay and myself to sit in with him while he was meeting managers of local employment exchanges to tell them what he wanted. Sam Chaloner, ever a believer in a satisfied Press, may have been partly responsible for this. But the marvel was that Bevin was so responsive.

One Friday evening Ian Mackay, Frank Machin of the *Daily Herald* and I were finishing a meal at the County Hotel, Durham, when Ernest Bevin, accompanied by Sir Godfrey Ince, the Director-General of Manpower, and A. S. Frere, Director of Public Relations, walked into the dining-room. Each party made suitable gestures of surprise at seeing the other there—of all places in the world. Bevin and his party finished their meal, then joined us in a tiny saloon at the back of the hotel. So did Bill (now Sir William) Lawther, the miners' president, who then lived in Durham, and Sam Watson, the Durham miners' leader.

It was a relaxed and affable party. Bevin and Ian did most of the talking, with an interjected reminiscence from Bill Lawther while the other two paused for breath. The most silent man there was Godfrey Ince, that remarkable man who planned Britain's mobilisation and who carries statistics in his head better than most Chancellors of the Exchequer. There is nothing forbidding or sinister about his silences. He is no skeleton at any feast. He just prefers listening. There he was, swirling the stem of his goblet which contained orange juice, smiling at the sallies, and sometimes roaring heartily at the retorts. But otherwise silent.

Bevin suddenly announced he was going to bed. He was walking out of the room, escorted by Ince and Frere, when Ian shouted after him, "Oh, Ernie!" Bevin wheeled around. Ian went on, "Whatever you do, stop Godfrey Ince babbling —we'll have no secrets left if he goes on chattering this way." Bevin's delighted roar almost shook the hostelry, and no one laughed more heartily than Ince. The most remarkable feature of this incident, however, was Ian's observation. We all thought he had been too busy talking to notice anyone else.

It was late the following night when Bevin told Ian,

Freddie Chant and me that he would hold a Press conference in the Station Hotel, Newcastle, at nine o'clock the next morning. "Sunday?" Ian queried. Bevin nodded. "Have a heart, Ernie, we'll hardly be in bed by then," Ian chuckled. Bevin explained that he was going down the Tyne early to inspect the shipyards, and he had a series of conferences and meetings throughout the day. He added, "It'll have to be nine or nothing." I put in, "Well, it had better be good." Bevin winked. "Tell me after its over," he suggested, and ambled off to rejoin the Lord Mayor.

Bevin looked over his spectacles as we trooped in disconsolately to his "Sunday niner," as he called it. He was buoyant. "I bet you chaps'll never forgive me for this," he chuckled. I retorted, "We'll wait until the end of the conference." Then calmly he broke one of the most important stories of the war. It was the first announcement of the part women were to play as civilians in the defence of Britain. The first call was for 100,000 women volunteers, partly for the munition factories, partly to replace men in subsidiary industries. "Any complaints?" grinned Bevin, looking at us meaningly.

Of course, every national newspaper "led" with the story next morning. The general headline was "Bevin wants 100,000 women." There followed each newspaper's "by-line." So, with hurried reading, the impression was given that he wanted them from each newspaper's own representative in Newcastle. Thus, the *News Chronicle* announced, "Bevin wants 100,000 women—From Ian Mackay, Newcastle, Sunday." Bevin could never pronounce the name Ian. But we knew what he meant when he cracked later "I hope Iron will let me have 100,000 of his women."

Ian had reason to remember a later ministerial tour. It was when Lord Beaverbrook, then Minister of Supply, went to Glasgow one weekend to hold a mass meeting with

Clydeside shop stewards to find out what was holding up production. Lord Beaverbrook had let it be known he was prepared to answer any questions put to him. It showed plenty of courage, for only two or three months earlier these same shop stewards had given a hostile reception to a Socialist Minister. They were in a truculent mood, and were contemptuous of orders from London. Yet here was Lord Beaverbrook holding his meeting in public in a Govan cinema. This was no meeting to be missed, whichever way it went!

I was with Lord Beaverbrook on the journey to Glasgow. Ian was travelling up on a later sleeping train, but we had arranged to join up at the meeting. It was an exciting affair. The arc lights of the news-reel projectionists were there too. The shop stewards had plenty to say, and they said it pungently. Lord Beaverbrook stood up to this barrage for nearly two hours, until there were no more questions to be answered It was a remarkable triumph, with even a vote of thanks thrown in by the shop stewards to make complete their appreciation of Beaverbrook's performance. Ian murmured to me during the meeting, "The old man's pulled another rabbit out of his hat."

Ian came round later that evening, after he had put his story over, to congratulate Lord Beaverbrook on his success. We were walking up the hotel stairs to Beaverbrook's rooms, when I looked suddenly at Ian and demanded, "What's different about you?" He stared at me in surprise. I insisted there was some change in him. He searched his body. "No," I insisted, "it's something about your face." He felt his face and then collapsed against the wall in mirth. When he laughed the secret was out.

"It's my teeth," he chortled. "I've lost my dentures. No, I'll tell you what happened. I forgot them—in the sleeping compartment. That's where they are."

"Do you mean to say," I demanded, "that you haven't missed them until now?" He said, "Why should I? They're only for show, anyway. I usually take them out to eat, when I eat. Don't let's bother." And on we went to meet Lord Beaverbrook. Ian didn't bother to reclaim his dentures. He explained he had never taken to them anyway. He got more used to his next set, but it took him some weeks to visit a dentist.

Ian had an unqualified success when he captured the hearts of part of the Soviet Navy. That was at Edinburgh in June 1944. We were attending an engineers' conference. A Soviet warship was at Leith and her crew had been given a short shore leave. As we walked into the bar of the George Hotel there were four or five Soviet sailors drinking beer. Ian stood in his tracks. There was a gleam in his eye. He strode over to the sturdy little fellow who appeared to be the leader of the party, and shooting his hand out, called, "Tovarich!" The little Russian beamed, and replied, "Tovarich." Excitedly the sailor obviously told his mates that here was a friend. So Ian solemnly shook hands with each of them, repeating the whole of his Russian vocabulary, "Tovarich." It was all Tovarich for the next minute, as the rest of us joined the party.

Then one of us insisted on buying a round. So we had two rounds—and two more, and two more. We got fed up just repeating Tovarich. So Ian raised his glass to toast, "Joe Stalin." "Ah," the sailors cried delightedly, "Tovarich Stalin." So Ian proposed another toast, "Winston Churchill." "Ah," the Russians repeated with pleasure, "Tovarich Churchill." Ian murmured, "And I bet that's one of the few times Winston has been toasted as Tovarich in an English— begging its pardon—a Scots pub."

Genial though we all were, this business of tovarich was beginning to pall. We have never consumed so much on such a limited vocabulary. The sailor Ian had first greeted seemed to sense this. So to widen the range of our talk he pointed to himself and said, "Dmitri." The next was Vassili, who had an impressive sprinkling of gold in his teeth. Then came Georgi, Josef and Ivan. We gave our names, which the Russians tried to repeat with some difficulty and much hilarity—until strictly applied licensing laws broke up the party. We saw them off the premises and hoped as they wove their unsteady way, arm in arm, down George Street that a lenient view of their geniality would be taken when they made ship.

When the cold war broke, Ian would often sigh, "If only we could have another jolly night with our old pals Dmitri and Vassili, and d'you know a funny thing?—maybe they think the same about us from time to time."

Then it happened.

Ian started complaining of "pain amidships." At last he was induced to visit a doctor. The old knight of the Anti-Luncheon League had been brought down. At 8.35 p.m. on October 25th, 1944, he was forced on the water-wagon by doctor's orders. The era of the beaker of bismuth had dawned.

Few people, especially victims, have a good word to say about duodenal trouble, with its restrictions and prohibitions and regimented diet and discomfort and pain. Usually it lacerates the body and humiliates the spirit. But not so with Ian. Of course he had pain and was sometimes depressed, but the main impact of his illness on him was novelty. His sense of humour was stimulated by the "comical caper" of having to munch a biscuit every two hours, he a man who for more than forty years had been recklessly and blatantly indifferent to solid food.

About ten minutes before the hour of mastication was due, Ian would pretend to get restless with eagerness. "Only ten

minutes before I can nibble my luscious charcoal biscuit,"
he would gurgle. And then, on the hour, he would announce
with delight, "Boys, we're off," and out of his pocket he
would fish an unappetising biscuit. He would make grateful
noises of contented and uninhibited pleasure, like a man
arriving in Dublin and letting himself go on a juicy man-size
steak after years of rationing in England. "Mind you," Ian
would assure us, "what I like about this diet is that I can
vary it. Sometimes I can have a crust of dry bread instead of
a biscuit!"

But the change in Ian's habits was profound. There
wasn't much point in pubs any more. Not that Ian didn't
trust himself if he went into a saloon. Dr. Henry Jacobs, of
St. John's Wood, had seen to that. He had adopted shock
tactics with a pencil on his writing pad to prove to Ian how
many minutes a double Scotch would knock off his life. And
Ian, the lover of life and company, was enthusiastic in his
fight against invalidism and death. The new régime, however,
created a mighty vacuum in his life. All those glorious hours
of carefree, sometimes brilliant, talk had to be abandoned
for the time being. What could take their place—for Ian was
never a lie-abed? Why, reading and walking—not country
walking, but city prowling. Any city, but preferably London,
for, as Ian said and wrote, the smell of asphalt burners in the
Strand was like the perfumes of Arabia to him.

His delight was to inspect the plaques and tablets com-
memorating the residences of illustrious or notorious
citizens, to relive in his imagination episodes from their
lives, and, by way of variation, kick up a fuss if he discovered
some worthy's former home without a plaque.

And reading. How he read. From the days he left the army
in what he always called "The Kaiser's War" he had devoted
at least three hours a day to reading, to reading everything
with only two daily constants, the newspapers and a page of

Shakespeare. Now he stepped up his reading to six hours a day. There was nothing mechanical about this. He loved lapping up the written word. To this he brought the priceless equipment of his prodigious memory, a memory flexible enough to file what he might want to recall and to note where to look for something which might elude him later.

So by the end of that winter of 1944-5, the last winter of the war, he was simply bursting with new knowledge, new interests, new enthusiasms and an urge to seek fresh outlets for his growing energy. Certainly his old job did not fill the bill, for he had been joined on the *News Chronicle* by the able and energetic Margaret Stewart, who ultimately succeeded him as the newspaper's industrial correspondent—the first woman to occupy this post on a national morning newspaper.

It was at Blackpool, during that hectic conference of the Labour Party which decided to end the wartime association with Churchill, that Ian first toyed with the idea of breaking new ground journalistically. Some Labour leaders, who may not realise it, helped enormously in this decision. For there was a pulsating, crusading air even in the cosy midnight groups who talked and argued in corners of hotel lounges from St. Anne's right up to Fleetwood. There was so much humility, too. There had not been an election for ten years, and a new, courageous, war-tried generation would be voting for the first time and had to be weighed by older men conscious of the dangers of both unfulfillable promises and uninspired caution. There was candour, too, the candour born of doubts about the result of the inevitable general election. And from this humility and candour came friendliness, untrammelled by the pomposity which the cares of State sometimes deposit on the souls of smaller politicians who are called to office from time to time.

The defences were down in the trusted confines of these

intimate circles. The best and highest men in the Party took time off to think aloud. And that was in a week when despatch riders were racing through the night between Churchill in Downing Street to Attlee, still deputy Prime Minister, in his private Blackpool suite, with offers and rejections of a postwar Coalition Government. Herbert Morrison, Morgan Phillips, Aneurin Bevan, Manny Shinwell, Hugh Dalton, Ernest Bevin and Arthur Greenwood (Arthur Greenwood, the dearest of Britain's public men, who had a special niche in the inner sanctum of Ian's most cherished friendships) all yarned with us that week.

"Do you know," Ian mused after one of these sessions, clutching his orange juice with well-mastered distaste, "there is much more in politics than our infernally scrappy newspapers will ever allow us to convey to the public?" He developed the idea. Obviously we could not reveal what we had been told in these private talks throughout the week. That would have been a betrayal of confidence, and the rupture of old and valued friendships. "No," Ian agreed, "we couldn't do that, but we could project what so many leaders feel deeply about without embarrassing them. And it could be done only in newspapers not hostile to them. Yet, it couldn't be done in the straight news columns. There isn't space, for one thing. And for another it would be difficult to avoid committing the newspaper to one's own ideas."

We were witnessing the birth pangs of a newspaper column which was to make Ian Mackay the most distinctive newspaper writer of his time.

As soon as we returned to London the date of the General Election was announced, July 5th, 1945—less than a month to go. Ian stopped Gerald Barry (now Sir Gerald), then editor of the *News Chronicle*, in an office corridor one day, and diffidently put up his scheme for an election commentary. "Come and talk to me in my office," Barry replied encouragingly. They went, and the more Ian talked the more he convinced himself that there was something in it. At last Barry laughed, "Go and have a shot, but, remember, we are a Liberal newspaper."

And Ian went. It wasn't so much an election column as a rediscovery of England through the eyes of a man whose erudition was constantly being poked in the eye by his whimsy, whose hopes for tomorrow were always giving way to his reverence for the past. There were nights in the office when Noel Joseph, the executive in charge, scratched his head and wondered if some of this stuff wasn't a bit too far removed from election comment. But it was so darned readable. It shrieked for publication, and the philosophical Noel would sigh, "Well, I suppose if it intrigues me it'll do the same to others." And it did. In a massive way.

Gerald Barry was captivated. He ordered Ian to widen the scope of the column when the election was over. How Ian leapt at the chance. More and more he withdrew from his industrial work, though he never lost interest in it. More and more Margaret Stewart assumed full responsibility for it, until at last the break was complete. Ian became a columnist and essayist in a full-time and magnificent way.

At first he called his column, "My bit of nonsense." He was almost apologetic about it. It took him a long time to realise the delight he gave the public, which is quick to report its disapproval, particularly of an inaccuracy, and so slow to say thank you.

And there were a fair number of inaccuracies in the early days of the column, partly because Ian set about his task with slapdash enthusiasm. As Stanley Baron, his colleague who so lovingly and skilfully edited the volume of Ian's selected columns and essays, recalls it, Ian once retorted when the veracity of some of his statements was challenged,

"It's not the truth which matters so much as the feeling behind the truth." But he became more experienced, more polished. He took enormous care to verify and recheck his references and allusions. Next to his faithful leaky pen, which he felt he would basely betray if he ever attempted to use such a contraption as a typewriter, his most valued tools were the encyclopædias, the reference books, the dictionaries, the verse collections, the gazetteers, and the anthologies. Not that he ever became the slave of any of them. He was their master, the craftsman who paid them the compliment of permitting them to become his instruments.

It has been estimated that he wrote a million words in his columns and his essays. Four years after he became a columnist he became an essayist, succeeding on his newspaper the shy, sensitive Robert Lynd. This gave Ian the distinction he valued most in life. The mantle of a great race, from Addison down through Chesterton, had become his inheritance, and *mirabile dictu*, it fitted perfectly. He was overjoyed. The compass to which John Vernon Ratcliffe had referred ten years before had been discovered. His journeyings had a direction.

What a metamorphosis there was from industrial writer to essayist. Robin Cruikshank, the editor of the *News Chronicle*, comments in *The Real Mackay*: "There was no one to prophesy that the best newspaper diarist and essayist of our time was buttoned up inside the man who was so knowledgeable about trade union practice and Labour relations."

No one indeed. Nor was that to be wondered at, for there were times as an industrial correspondent when Ian would not scorn the comfortable escape of a cliché. Yet this was the same man who, in a little-noticed escape into reminiscence before the war, had written of his boyhood in Wick: "There was I, a melancholy moon circling round and round in a monotonous orbit—making zinc ointment and linseed poultices—when I wanted to be a flaming comet rushing away into the infinite. It took me years to learn that comets, too, have their prescribed orbits and come back at last as regularly as the moon."

And the man who wrote years later of a coloured quack dentist who used to visit Wick: "His skull, which was smooth and shiny as a black billiard ball, was fringed with lambswool curls, and when he laughed his teeth glimmered like snowdrops in a crimson cave."

It was the later Ian Mackay, too, who wrote: "I have always looked upon Burlington Bertie as a contemporary of mine, the kind of chap I might have been if I had been unlucky enough to be born at the top with nowhere to go but down instead of at the bottom with nowhere to go but up."

Yes, the shining light of a star had taken nearly half a century to travel from remote Wick to Fleet Street, but once its glimmer had been observed we had the delight of seeing it gleam before our very eyes until its incandescence warmed our hearts.

Ian himself changed slightly with his growing fame and stature. He mellowed, but that might have been the inevitable toll of the years and of his goaded duodenum, and he was better dressed, and that was the influence of Rosemary-known-as-Pat Say whom he married in mid-1951. But he never wore a hat—except, of course, his wonderful runcible. This was presented to him by Mr. Battersby himself, who explained, "The best runcibles, being five-dimensional, can be perceived only by the intellect, and the clarity of the perception is dependent on the magnitude of the intellect."

Other people may not have noticed that incredible five-dimensional runcible perched on his still luxurious, grey-flecked, better-trimmed thatch, but Ian himself was

MOOD DIDACTIC

—*by Illingworth.*

aware of it, particularly if we went into low-raftered places like mining galleries or the cellars of old country pubs, for as we bent down Ian would murmur, "That gave me a nasty jab in the runcible." His wedding reception was one of the great milestones in Ian's career. In addition to Rosemary-known-as-Pat's family, with their representatives in the Services and the Church, there were politicians a-plenty, and his own office was well mustered under the genial leadership of Robin Cruikshank. Vivian Brodzky and Paula, my wife and I were there.

Some time during the afternoon, Ian nudged Brod and me into a corner, and grasping the lapel of his resplendent new suit, the most beautifully cut he had ever worn, he simpered as he pirouetted, "Aren't I a gorgeous beast?—bet you hardly recognised me, 'cept for my beak." But it was a shock to Brod and me a few minutes later when a *News Chronicle* secretary came up to us and said, "Of course, you two are the only relics of his old days here!" She had recognised the great divide in Ian's career.

Late on a Saturday in September 1952, before the Labour Party's annual conference opened at Morecambe, Ian burst into the spacious lounge of the Euston Hotel there. Brodzky and I were in a circle chatting to Arthur Deakin, Tom O'Brien and Sir William Lawther. He came for me like an arrow, and declared, almost accusingly, "I haven't a bed in which to rest my weary bones this night." This had happened so many times before over the years that I answered, "O.K. Relax and sit down."

He was soon giving us a graphic description of his journey up from London that day. He had been driven up by Desmond Hirshfield, a well-known accountant interested in the Labour and trade union movements, and his wife Bronia. They had been hours and hours overdue because Ian was "navigator" and he wanted to show them "some of the loveliest corners" of the North, which had meant zigzagging across the West Riding, Derbyshire and Lancashire. "I wouldn't have sacrificed a mile or a minute of it because Ian was in such cracking form," Desmond admitted later. And here was Ian, convulsing us with his dramatised version of the day's incidents.

It was early in the morning when he accompanied Brod and me back to the Clarendon Hotel, where Ian thought earlier that he had been booked in. He had discovered, however, that his office reservations were for the following night. Brod and I were sharing a huge double-bedded room, so it was easy and natural for me to offer Ian half my bed— but on one condition. I said, "It's two-thirty now—you can come in on condition talk ends at three-thirty." He grinned agreement. We compromised; lights were out and there was silence by 4.0 a.m. When we rose we discovered that the adjoining bedroom had remained unoccupied. It had been reserved in the name of Ian Mackay. In his modesty, Ian had inquired only for " a *News Chronicle* room."

What a mad, sad week that was. The bitterness which followed the shattering landslide of Bevanite victories on the National Executive, the remorse which followed the defeat of Herbert Morrison and Hugh Dalton, the resentment of some of the trade union leaders—all contributed to a conference which most Socialists will want to forget, despite some quiet sessions in the softly upholstered saloon of the Clarendon, which Ian characteristically referred to as "the padded cell."

It was all in acute contrast with previous Labour conferences, particularly the one in Blackpool eight years earlier. Then we could talk to anyone in "a great big happy family"; now we had to mind where we talked to whom. It would be tactless, for example, to be too closely closeted with Bevanites in the presence of more orthodox officials. And

vice versa. Brotherhood was at a discount. So we escaped
into the sanity of our own padded cell.

There, at least, it was restful to chat with Lord Winster
about current art trends in Cyprus and Australia, with Sir
Leslie Plummer about the prospects of food production in
Queensland, and with Frank Bowles, M.P., about the
wittiest parliamentary interjections any of us could recall.

But the most precious sessions of all were held when most
of the tormented politicians had ceased their strife and were,
no doubt fitfully, asleep. Ian preferred talk to sleep, the
inconsequential, unforced talk between old friends which
can of itself be so restful. He and I had one long-standing
secret which would always be dragged out on such occasions.
Our Greek Club.

This was a very exclusive affair; so exclusive that not even
its members knew they belonged to it. It was so christened
because Ian said it would be amusing to see what really
happens "when Greek meets Greek." So we decided to elect
to our nebulous Greek Club the people we loathed. And the
degree of our loathing would be reflected in the positions we
allocated to them in the club. Thus, the currently most
contemptible man would be president, and then would come
the three vice-presidents, and people who were just bores but
otherwise harmless would be ordinary members. It was
always a very small club. Neither of us had many hates, nor
were we malicious, so our Greek Club never had more than
a dozen members at any one time, and few presidents held
the job longer than three successive years.

"Met any Greeks lately?" Ian inquired. There were no
new ones, and indeed we released one man from membership.
It turned out he wasn't such a bad chap, after all. And from
chatting about the people we didn't like, it was inevitable
that the talk would drift to those we did. Here there would
be real enthusiasm, particularly if the name of someone like

Arthur Greenwood cropped up. He was faultless in our eyes. Even what some regarded as his shortcomings, such as his lack of thrust when he had the ball at his feet fifteen years earlier, were virtues to us.

And then Ian's talk would go off at a tangent. "I bet Arthur Moyle wouldn't do this week what he did in Scarborough a couple of years back," he challenged. I agreed hastily. That was a memorable incident. The cheerful Arthur Moyle was Parliamentary Private Secretary to Mr. Attlee, when Labour's chief was Prime Minister. And one evening while the Party was holding its annual conference at Scarborough, Arthur Moyle approached Ian and me in the Grand Hotel to inform us that "the chief" would like to meet us. Mr. Attlee, he said, knew all the political correspondents, but he knew only the work of the industrial correspondents. Could we meet him for a chat and a drink about ten o'clock? "But mind," Arthur warned, "no politics."

Now here was a problem. If politics were barred what could we talk about? Books, suggested Ian. I thought America would be a neutral enough topic at that time. "Bound to get back to politics that way," Ian countered. So I retorted that seeing Attlee had asked to meet us, he could open the conversation and we would follow. That's how it worked out. Promptly at ten o'clock Attlee stalked down the magnificent stairs at the Grand Hotel, which look like the backcloth to the finale of a Drury Lane show. Talk in the crowded lounge tailed off until it was no louder than the buzz of a dozen bees. Five hundred eyes watched the Prime Minister's progress as he came nearer. He veered to the right at the bottom of the stairs, and went through the swing doors to an empty table with seats for four, which had been placed within the curve of a glass partition.

Arthur Moyle, having seen the Prime Minister seated, and

settling to fill his pipe from his pouch, scuttled across the lounge to Ian and myself, who were straightening our ties in the corridor and feeling as bashful as little girls about to sing their first duet at a village concert. We could almost hear eyes popping out of their sockets as we marched self-consciously in the wake of the brisk Arthur Moyle. And after we had ordered whisky ("I'll give my duodenum a treat as well," Ian whispered), it was Clem Attlee who set the theme by asking if we had seen the overnight cricket scores from India—or was it South Africa?

It was cricket, cricket all the time. And what an expert Attlee turned out to be. There wasn't a cricketing topic he couldn't amplify—even to the detailed performances of such pioneers of my own county, Glamorgan, as Nash, Creber and Norman Riches, whose careers were ending when I first became a regular, devoted and sometimes anguished supporter of the club.

We ordered another round. And turning to Ian, Attlee mused about the failure of the game to take a hold in Scotland, and then went on to add to Ian's proud list of Scots who have been great cricketers. We ordered another drink. And then Attlee proceeded to demonstrate the secret of Larwood's spin by placing his thumb and third finger in the right position, and swinging his right arm over to start the delivery. I saw over his shoulder that amazement crept into the eyes of the curious observers in the lounge beyond the glass partition. One confessed later he hoped Attlee was going to clip us on the ears! It was a happy, carefree, unselfconscious half-hour. We had difficulty in persuading our colleagues that we hadn't taken advantage of the occasion to scoop them. Attlee's imitation of Larwood helped.

But that night in Morecambe in the late September of 1952 Ian sighed, "Poor old Attlee's got too much on his plate this week to think about cricket." Suddenly Ian demanded, "How long did it take you to write your biography of Ernie Bevin?" I replied, "Six crazy weekends." He mused, "I can't spare weekends because of my broadcasts in Scotland. But I must get down to it. I think I'll take some of my holidays about Christmas—they owe me a couple of weeks from 1950—and go and lock myself up in a snow-bound farm with Pat and all the material."

For years he had been collecting material about the life of one of his greatest heroes, Ben Tillett. "Remember when we ran across old Ben in Bristol?" he asked. It was in the early days of the war. We were in Bristol on one of those Ministry of Labour tours. We were in the middle of breakfast when a pained voice from the next table called out, "So you don't recognise your old pals when you are out of London?" It was Ben. He had been speaking in Bristol the night before for the Ministry of Information. The old orator was in good mood because he had recaptured some of his old fire of fifty years earlier. It was his breakfast we always remembered— a bottle of Scotch ale and two kippers! And he was nearly eighty.

Ian was haunted by his procrastination on the Tillett book. He kept repeating, "I must get down to it. It won't take long once I start. It's all in my head." He planned it as a masterpiece. And what a masterpiece it would have been, with Ben's rich and fruitful life and Ian's inspired imagery.

That touches the most tragic note of all. For Ian Mackay left us on the threshold of his greatest intentions.

PART TWO

The Boyhood of
Ian Mackay

BY

HERBERT SINCLAIR

Herbert Sinclair, now living in semi-retirement in Wick, founded his own publishing business, which specialises in musical publications, notably The Pianomaker.

I N the calm of an early October evening in 1952, as I was walking down my garden path in Wick, where Ian Mackay was born, the voice of my next-door neighbour came to me, "Ian Mackay is dead. The news has just been broadcast." And there by myself, in the darkening of the night, I stood and let my mind go back; saddened by the passing of one who was more to me than a friend.

Now I am sitting in front of a typewriter half a mile from the birthplace of Ian Mackay in that part of Wick known locally as Whitechapel. And I am setting down the gleanings of my research into that restless red-headed laddie with the unquenchable thirst for book knowledge.

Ian Mackay and I were both born in Wick. I left the town when he was five years old. And, after forty-five years in London, I returned in 1948 to the scenes of my nativity—to use a phrase popular with Ian. So the privilege has been given me of writing about his boyhood days and the years he spent with me in London.

At the time of Ian Mackay's birth, Wick was still one of the chief herring-fishing centres in Scotland, although once it had been the leading port of them all. During the summer herring fishing, the population was almost doubled by fishermen and women workers from England, the Morayshire coast, the North-west coast of Scotland and the Hebrides. On Saturday nights the two main streets of the town were crowded with the "stranger" fisher folk walking up and down, and in the harbour the congestion of steam drifters and fishing boats was such that boys could cross the Inner Harbour by passing from one vessel to another—as Ian Mackay often did. The herring fishing gave employment to thousands of women, and Ian's mother was one of them.

About Midsummer Day there is daylight in Wick almost to midnight, then follows a slight darkening, and then the dawn. The air of Caithness is bracing, and when the sun shines Caithness is a bonnie countryside with wide stretches of undulating pastures and moors, bounded by grand rock scenery. But in winter? Wick is then a little grey town. Cold and drab. The days are short and the nights long, and in Ian Mackay's boyhood, when there was neither cinema nor radio, winter was the time for reading; and he was the most earnest reader of them all.

When a boy, Robert Louis Stevenson spent some time in Wick, while his engineer father, Thomas Stevenson, was trying to build Wick's ill-fated breakwater. The attempt ended in failure, and perhaps because of that catastrophe Robert Louis Stevenson described Wick as "the meanest of men's towns on the baldest of God's bays." Graphic, but untrue.

As I type there comes, wafted on the wind, the smell of burning heather and a sort of mist that settles on the town from the heights; on such an evening the young Ian Mackay would have been playing football on the Bleaching Green, a stretch of common land on the north side of Wick river, and near Whitechapel. The boys had not the money to buy a football, so, instead, they kicked a cork from a herring net—

a "corkie" they called it. At that sort of football Ian was a bit of a flyer, according to Dannie Sutherland. Dannie and Ian were playmates, and Dannie, by my fireside, says of him, "He wore a pair of strong boots, the soles of which carried many iron protectors. His stockings were heavy home-knitted. He had knickerbockers, and, on top, a gansey [jersey]. He had a head of dark red hair, cut straight across like that of a native of some South Sea island, but with two side whiskers like Robbie Burns."

Ian was a thin wisp of a lad who took big raking strides. In summer-time, when playing on the Bleaching Green, Ian would suddenly shout, "Who's for the Sandy Bankie?" Away up the river all would go until they reached that spot, beyond which there was a pool into which they dived from the Giant's Seat. Ian could never swim more than a few yards, but in the race on land back to the Bleaching Green he left his comrades far behind. When dribbling a corkie on the Bleaching Green he would be muttering poetry as he sped along, addressing the ball in somewhat different language to that in which golfers address the wee white ba'! On occasions, so Dannie Sutherland says, the language was something that Dannie did not understand, probably Latin; and when he would ask Ian what he was saying, the latter would give a small smile and play on. They usually played this kind of football after school and before tea; and just before six o'clock Ian would disappear into his house. Shortly afterwards he would reappear, with a piece of bread and jam in his hand, and make his way to the library, then presided over by George "Dodger" Bain.

No one seems to know what Ian read in the library, but when it closed shortly after nine, Ian would stride hastily home, and none of his playmates saw him again until the next morning. What did he do? He went to bed with a book.

Ian Mackay was a most earnest student at the University

of Literature, many portals of which are to be found in the libraries throughout Scotland, open to all through the generosity of Andrew Carnegie. Ian was always searching after book knowledge, and, by that meticulous probing into all the written avenues which lead to wisdom, he acquired something wider than any university could give—something which, coupled with a retentive memory, provided him with a ready answer on very many subjects. And that was the explanation I gave to Christopher Stone on a railway journey between Paddington and Birmingham, when he said he had never met a man with a wider general knowledge than Ian Mackay's, and asked me how he had acquired it. Just the ceaseless quest after the written word.

Was this flair for book knowledge hereditary? Well, according to Mrs. Macleod of Wick, Ian's mother was a remarkable woman. She left school at fourteen, maybe earlier, and was a worker for ever after. In the summer fishing season she was a herring worker, and at harvest time she went out in the fields. Her struggle to make ends meet and bring up her family of three boys was such that at the end of the fishing season when she lifted her earnings from her employer, the money all went to pay for food and other things which had to be bought during the weeks she was working at the herring. Her mother helped to balance the family budget by doing similar work. They had a hard struggle. There were never many pennies for sweets or anything beyond the necessities of existence. It was the remembrance of the grim struggle for existence that made Ian Mackay the true Socialist writer; he was of the people, and by the magic of his pen weaved his way into the hearts of the people.

Ian's mother, like her son, could not keep her hands off a book, and the more abstruse its nature, the more she seemed to like it. And so, this herring-and-farm girl could talk on almost any subject, like her son; from politics to the human body, from the stars to the earth's strata—a well-informed woman who, amid all her struggles to keep her family from being hungry, could rise above her straitened condition by the aid of books; and she seldom read fiction.

Ian went to two schools, West Banks and the Academy. And the end of his schooling days marked the end of the old type of headmaster, such as William Dick, rector of the Academy, whose name was a household word. Under him the scholars got a thorough grounding in the three Rs. While at school Ian got his first job, delivering newspapers after school, for a local stationer, Arthur Bruce. Never was there a more weird deliverer of newspapers. One of his school friends, Alex Weir, accompanied him at times on his rounds. To share in possible tips? No, just to hear Ian declaim some Shakespearian extract as they stopped at a corner while the people were waiting for their papers! You could hardly imagine an English messenger boy delaying his journey, in the midst of a snowstorm, maybe with a bitterly cold wind, so that he could pose as Hamlet.

Alex Weir also recalls the occasion when, standing at the deep end of the swimming pool on the North Shore, he was pushed into the water. He could not swim at all. Ian, not a good swimmer, immediately dived into the pool and brought his friend out. Ian was always ready to help. Arthur Bruce, son of the stationer who gave Ian his first job, remembers when he and Ian were in a hired boat on the river. They were in shallow water when they heard the afternoon train toot its approach to Wick. Over sprang Ian into the water. "Come on, or we'll be late for the train." Both of them waded the river, climbed the brae to the railway station—and Ian's newspapers were delivered in time.

It was Arthur Bruce who also told me the story about Ian, at a later date, being sent with an urgent delivery of medicine by the chemist for whom he acted as message boy. On his way, he went into the library, found a book he liked and hours afterwards he was found reading it in a shed. Out of his mind were both Willie Gow Miller, the chemist, and his sickly customer.

When he was fourteen Ian left school to take up his job with Willie Gow Miller of the Pharmacy, Wick. Gow Miller had the Pickwickian touch—a beaming round face, a pair of twinkling eyes, a slightly rotund figure, and a genial manner. After Ian had been some time with him, and had advanced to the dispensing department, unqualified, it was Willie Gow Miller's intention to send him to study medicine at Aberdeen University and defray all expenses.

But the first world war came, and at the age of seventeen Ian joined up, giving his age as nineteen, and became a stretcher bearer attached to the Irish Brigade. Before that Willie Gow Miller would send Ian out with medicine, and this is what often happened. Ian would have the basket on one arm, a book in the other, and people steered out of his way as he walked along. Sometimes he would stop, lean a shoulder against a house, cross his legs, and read more comfortably. It was all the same if he went to Oldwick to fetch the chemist's lunch—in the basket in which medicine was delivered. On the way he would meander slowly through the streets, with basket and book, but on the way back those strides of his could not be quick enough to ensure that the meal should be hot when it was delivered in Bridge Street.

The library was not the only centre of knowledge he frequented. In Lower Dunbar Street in Pulteneytown, then part of Wick, was a stationer's shop owned by John George and Son, and there was a branch in Bridge Street. In that Lower Dunbar Street shop was a young assistant, Harriet Dunnett, who is now in the Bridge Street shop, though it is under different ownership. She has many memories of

"Johnnie," as she calls him, and there is a softness in her voice whenever she talks to me about him. For they were great friends for many a day. When he was over in France Ian used to write her long letters, descriptive and thrilling, which, it is her one regret now, she did not preserve. Her mother used to say to her, "Johnnie's letters are spoiling you for other boys." So she is still unmarried, and ready to talk to me at any time about this friend of her youth, and eager to hear stories about his time with me in London.

Into the Lower Dunbar Street shop used to walk the bold Mackay, shoulders thrown back, and with a shock of red hair that periodically needed the attention of his right hand, as restlessly he paced up and down, exchanging views on news or books, or expressing Left political beliefs. In those days the works of Shakespeare were the Bible to him, and, says Miss Dunnett, he was word perfect in a manner that would make leading London actors astonished—this schoolboy of not yet fourteen years. They would go out on walks in the evening, Ian, Harriet Dunnett and two others. And the stars in the sky were as familiar to him as later were the stars in the political firmament. His companions stood and wondered when he told them the story of the heavens. Just a mere boyagie, as we call a young laddie in this part of Scotland.

To his capacity for memorising poetry there is this tribute of another school friend, Charles Begg: "At one time Tennyson's 'In Memoriam' was his masterpiece, and you could shut your eyes and almost make yourself believe you were listening to the Lincolnshire-born poet himself giving you one of his best."

In reply to a paragraph about the preparation of this book in the *John O'Groat Journal*—which published Ian's first efforts—three letters were sent me. This was from John Duncan, a lifelong Liberal advocate in Wick:

"Though it must have been in 1909 or thereabouts, it seems but yesterday that the incident occurred. I was homeward bound in the early evening of a summer day. The road was quiet and the atmosphere disturbed only by the noise of a 'spanker.' This is the local name of a two-wheeled barrow the boy was now pushing along the macadamised roadway. He was then 'prentice to W. Gow Miller, The Pharmacy, Wick, and was quite well known to me as a somewhat lanky loon of twelve or so with a head of hair the colour of bronze. (I was perhaps ten years his senior.) He slowed down as he came abreast of me, looked across with his keen, rather expectant expression and shouted, 'What d'you think o' Asquith now?' "

What Asquith said or did in 1909 I do not remember, but here was the young Socialist of twelve years, ready to have a dig at the Liberal stalwart! The letter went on:

"The last time I met him was while travelling south by the Highland Railway. Sometime between the wars. We met in the corridor; he took me into his compartment and introduced me to Mr. Templeton, M.P. They had attended a garden party at Dunrobin Castle. I was entertained to a lot of interesting talk and noticed that the only occasions on which the M.P. spoke was at 'question time.' Ian Mackay was still interested in politics."

Of Ian's schooldays there came a remembrance from Miss J. Cormack: "We were in the same class at school, and one little incident I have never forgotten. Our class was meeting in the West Church Hall as the High School had not then been completed. A lesson in mathematics was in progress, with the teacher busy writing on the blackboard with her back towards the class. Taking advantage of this we pupils were throwing at one another the missiles pupils usually throw on such an occasion. Suddenly the teacher

turned and said 'John Mackay, put that where you got it.'
" 'Miss, I got it in the eye!' was his quick reply."

Another episode was described to me by Ian's brother
Willie, who lives in Edinburgh. When the family were
having tea one evening the cry went up, "A lassie's in the
river." Ian ran down the stairs, sped across the Bleaching
Green, jumped into the river, brought the wee lassie to
safety, and then slipped away to the chemist's shop, wet as
he was up to the thighs. Willie was told by his mother that
when Ian was about six she found him yelling his head off,
with an empty sweet bag in his hand, and surrounded by a
lot of pleased youngsters. He had dished out all the sweeties
and had left none for himself. Willie ended his letter: "Ian
was always a bookworm, and a book seemed to come before
his food, for he always read at meals. By the time he joined
the army, he had accumulated about 1,300 of the 6d. and
7d. editions published by Nelson's, Ward Lock's and
Collins'."

One day, soon after the first world war, Ian went over to
his friend Harriet Dunnett, and from his pockets he produced the best of his treasured books, giving them to her as
a keepsake of the days when they were boy and girl friends.
Then, pawning his brother Willie's camera—with permission—to raise the fare, he took the train south.

My Brother Jock

HUGH MACKAY

*Hugh Mackay, Ian Mackay's brother, is an executive of one of the
leading firms of advertising consultants.*

MY most vivid memories of Ian—I always called him
Jock—had little to do with his later fame. Not that
fame altered him at all. It did not. It was middle-
age, not distinction, which mellowed his appearance—but
not his rebellious mind. The frequent twinkle in his eye
proved that.

I always liked the way that Jock became a crony of all the
old folk in Wick when he was quite young. He used to be a
great follower of a shiftless old wanderer named Ericey
Chancer who was known as "Chipping Gong." The more
worthy townsfolk scorned Chipping Gong, but Jock taught
my brother Willie and me to adore the drunken roll of the
explosive but harmless old man.

Every Sunday Jock used to read to our Grannie from the
Old Testament. She stuck to Isaiah, Ezekieh and Job and
was positively a Hebrew in her refusal to come to the more
modern prophecies of the New Testament, which she might
have described in a later day as the *No Orchids for Miss
Blandish* of the Holy Scripture.

Jock used to read to her—one minute in the dreary moan
of the Clochers' minister with "hielan" intonation, then in
the thundering voice of some good man from the Wee Frees.
Then he would imitate the Rev. Mr. Peebles. When he got
tired of that he would deliver the message in the tones of an

outrageous sinner like Chipping Gong, and Grannie would beat him.

Another of Jock's favourite tricks was to read into the Bible a report from the *Groat* of the Academy *v.* Thistle match: "And Bolta Nicolson came down on the fold like a football match Assyrian wolf, swinging the ball out to the wing for Chonny Christie. . . ." Then, too, there would be trouble.

Jock was keen on football. He was a first-rate speedy outside right who, but for the war and his passion for journalism, may well have developed into professional class.

And his Bible readings served him well. He often told me that when he first got to London he wrote sermons and sold them to ministers at two guineas each.

He was violently hostile to drink before he left Wick. I remember he swore to my mother that he would never touch a drop of the stuff. But he was no sooner in London than he won notoriety by leading a students' rag against "Pussyfoot" Johnson, who was preaching prohibition. Jock jumped on to "Pussyfoot's" platform and delivered an impromptu harangue on the crying need for more drink for all.

I still recall the mixture of awe and sorrow I felt on hearing what my brother would do as a free lance journalist to get new experiences which could be turned into saleable copy. He got a pilot to fly him between the towers of Tower Bridge. And he looped the loop over London when this performance was still a novelty.

Years later, when he was becoming an established newspaper writer, he had a phase of carefree boyishness. Once in a Brighton hotel, the Cricketers Arms, Jock was among a party of reporters who came in late and merry after a Press conference that had been continued in the local pubs. And Jock was the ringleader in disarranging the shoes outside each bedroom door. He put a pair of men's shoes beside every pair of ladies' and rang the changes by putting men's at ladies' doors and vice versa.

Next morning the hotel was in an uproar with angry guests clamouring for their shoes and old spinsters protesting no knowledge of the men's shoes which were laid alongside their own. The hotel manager happened to have a keen sense of fun, and once the chaos was straightened out he brought up a bottle of whisky to the reporters, saying he had never enjoyed himself so much since he gave up the music halls for hotcl-keeping.

How Ian Became a Londoner

BY

HERBERT SINCLAIR

SOMEBODY telephoned me that "Mac," who was writing a weekly column for the *John O'Groat Journal*, wanted to have a chat with me. "Mac" represented but a pen-name to me then, as he was not of my generation in our native town of Wick; all the same, just because he came from that town, he could call on me whenever he liked. So, one afternoon, into my office in Little Titchfield Street, W.1, walked John Cockburn Mackay, devoid of hat, maybe because it would take more than an outsize in hats to cover that head of hair.

Of the little town in the north we talked much, of the worthies, of the herring fishing and of the football clubs. He hesitated long before he came to the reason for his visit. Eventually, he blurted it out. He was trying to live in London on the Government grant to students at the London School of Economics, and it wasn't much of a life. His people were not in a position to help him, and whenever he tried to find part employment for afternoon work, there was no opening. Nothing much to which he could turn his hands, he admitted, except writing. If he could only continue his studies, he was sure he could make good. He did not ask me to find a place for him, and there was no vacancy, but I said he could come to us in the afternoons and be of general use.

Never was it a case of employer and employee. There was a bond between us because of our birthplace, and, maybe, in our natures we had a little in common. To me he was always "Mac," and to the end "Skipper" was the name he called me. I told him he was at perfect liberty to do what he liked; if it were inconvenient to come to the office any afternoon, that would not matter. And that is how Ian Mackay and I came together.

One of the very first things he told me about his earliest days in London was how he ran down the centre of Fleet Street with a cap between his teeth "just to let Fleet Street know I had arrived." He would, too, in those early days, talk about walking up and down Baker Street, trying to place the mythical address of Sherlock Holmes.

My office was a minute's walk from Pagani's Restaurant in Great Portland Street. This place was patronised by world-famed musical artists, music publishers, composers and piano-makers; and as my publishing business was associated with the music industry, I sat for years at the same table of this restaurant. Ian Mackay, joining me, liked the food—the most generous helpings in London, with double *entrecôte* steaks from Aberdeen, and Dover soles equal to any to be had anywhere.

Pagani's was run by Arthur Meschini and his mother, Linda. Arthur, known to thousands of people, took a fancy to Ian—perhaps because they both had a luxuriant growth of hair. More so, perhaps, because the young Scot had a likeable nature. At the time I was trying to establish a monthly musical magazine, the *Musician*, but it never hit popular fancy and was eventually absorbed by another publishing house. The great Tetrazzini was lunching in Pagani's one day, and I thought it was an opportunity to present her with a copy of the first issue. I sent Ian round to the office to bring a copy and asked Arthur Meschini to take

Ian up to the singer's table. Bending with the courtesy of a Polish count, the youth from Wick presented the copy with a flourish of the hand. Tetrazzini gazed at him for a second or so, and said something in Italian to Meschini. Arthur told me, "She asked me if he was a Russian anarchist, and said that she thought him droll."

Another time, years later, at Pagani's, Harry Vardon, six times open golf champion, was with us. We were going over to the Queen's Hall, where Tommy Milligan of Hamilton was fighting Kid Nitram of Paris, over twenty rounds; a fight won by Tommy in the nineteenth, as I remember. Next to our table were three Yorkshiremen, and they must have noticed the accent in which Ian and I talked. One of them said, intending us to hear, "A Scotsman is *so* mean that he doesn't even drop an aitch."

" 'ORRIBLE!" Ian cried out. And there was silence at the next table.

At the Queen's Hall that night Harry Vardon sat between us. Left-handed I am, and back would go my elbow into Harry's right ribs, as I followed Tommy Milligan's jabs, and on the other side, the bold Mackay was hitting the golf champion with his right elbow. When Harry Vardon got to South Herts Golf Club next day he told members that not even when being chased by Sandy Herd, James Braid and J. H. Taylor was he so much on edge as when sitting between "those two mad Scotsmen."

One week in the month was usually a lazy time in those Little Titchfield Street days. Sometimes a couple of singers from the Three Arts Club would come to lunch with me at Pagani's, and afterwards we would return to the office. Ian was great for a game of nap, and maybe his army days had quickened him in the art. Anyway, it wasn't he who lost the money. One afternoon when he had lifted pennies from three of us, I remember Bessie Kerr (aunt to Neil Paterson, the

Scottish author) saying, "Mac, if you are as slick with your pen as you are with your fingers, you will go far."

In the years before his death Ian became great friends with Neil Paterson, through their "A Matter of Opinion" broadcasts.

It was an easy sort of office we ran in Little Titchfield Street. Often we had lunch there instead of going out. At that time, on the right-hand side going down Charing Cross Road, there was a snack bar, where cuts from a nice, juicy red roast, or a bit of brisket of beef, or even half a chicken, could be had far cheaper than in a restaurant. Rayner's was the name I think.

I had invited two friends to join us one day, and I asked Ian to buy a cooked fowl on his way to the office, and be with us by one o'clock. One o'clock came but no Ian. Two o'clock passed, and I was apologetic. At the back of three, he strolled into the office with the fowl. Language was expressed which comes naturally to anyone born in a northern seaport. He made no apology. He said simply, "I just strolled into Foyle's, began handling books, and never thought of food." But having satisfied his literary hunger, his share of the fowl disappeared quickly.

About this time Ian stopped sending his weekly piece to the *John O'Groat Journal*, and addressed it instead to the *Northern Ensign*—a newspaper no longer in existence but which was then owned by Sir Leicester Harmsworth. I had helped Sir Leicester in the 1918 election when he was re-elected for Caithness, and so it was a lucky changeover for Ian—because later I was able to influence Harold and Bobby Harmsworth to ask their father to give Ian a chance on the *Western Morning News*.

The most thrilling paragraph Ian sent to the *Northern Ensign* was about a murder committed in the Bell public house, next door to my offices. A musician from Jamaica, with a job in a London orchestra, used a revolver on his blonde wife, and when she got to the outside door she collapsed in the arms of—Ian, whose clothes were covered with blood. The Jamaican then committed suicide. Ian's account of the tragedy was read by the boys of his native Whitechapel in Wick. That such things could happen! But such things happened often to Ian. He was then in diggings in Torrington Square, and had no previous experience of geysers. He almost closed the bathroom door one night and turned on the gas. It was not until some time later that he thought of applying a match. The bang, he said, sent him and the door outwards, and—listen to this—"I found myself in the arms of the landlady's daughter, to my dismay but to her evident joy."

One of my most vivid recollections of Ian—visualising him physically—was of a Saturday afternoon in the Æolian Hall. Some of us thought that what a foreign artiste was billed to enact came too soon after the end of the war and the upset of the whole world. So a demonstration was proposed, with Ian and a dozen students from the London School of Economics as the men of protest. Just before the hubbub quietened down, from my seat on the ground floor I caught sight of Ian's profile as he stood in the front row upstairs. That patrician nose of his was well in the air, like a Roman senator's; his upper lip was curled in scorn, and pieces of a torn programme dropped gently and demonstratively from his fingers.

Twice a week I used to watch boxing at the Ring, Blackfriars, when the popular George Harris, ten times worse than Jimmy Thomas with his aitches, was the central figure at half time. It was then he read or tried to read the boxing items for the next occasion, making a horrible job of the names of foreign boxers. Purposely, sometimes, to get the crowd's laugh. Ian and I were at the Ring one night when

A BREAKFAST MEMORY
OF IAN , 1949

"WE'VE HEARD OF CHAPS WHO FOUND
SERMONS IN STONES BUT HERE'S A BLOKE
THAT FINDS ESSAYS IN POACHED EGGS"

CONVERSATION PIECE

—*by Low.*

two rows in front of us sat Sir Louis Greig. There was a New Zealand boxer in the ring, and, in a seat in front of us sat a New Zealander, who tapped Sir Louis on the shoulder, pointed to his compatriot in the ring, and said, "He killed a man in New Zealand." Sir Louis, with a slight turn of his head, threw over his shoulder the crack, "Was he a taxi-driver?" At which Ian threw himself back, and his body shook with laughter. The New Zealander in front turned angrily, and a row was avoided when I whispered that Ian was an ex-boxer, slightly punch-drunk, and that I was his keeper. But that New Zealand boxer, years later, got into trouble in America over a tragedy in the ring.

The first editor of the *Musician* was Dr. Henry Coates, who became music critic of the *Daily Chronicle*. One Saturday afternoon he had too many musical events to attend, and he deputed Ian Mackay to write something about open-air music in Hyde Park. Unfortunately, there was a demonstration of Old English Dancing in the Park the same day, and Ian went to the wrong event. There was puzzlement at first when the copy reached the *Chronicle*, but the quality of it was such that it was published on the Monday.

An invitation had come to both Ian and myself from John Horne, Caithness poet and author, to visit the Burns country. Horne, long resident in Ayr, was one of the trustees of the Burns Cottage and other relics. The only time I saw Ian wearing a hat was when he posed for a photograph with Horne at the head of the grave of Gavin Hamilton, the friend of Robert Burns. We were taken through the cottage, and met a woman caretaker with a cast in one eye. As we stood by the bed of Burns and Jean Armour, his wife—just the mere skeleton of the bed, with the rustic wood of Ayrshire where nowadays there would be springs—the caretaker touched one of the rungs and said with what was meant to be a naughty smile, "Rabbie lekt Nature."

Ian looked at her. "Aye, and just because of that, you're earning a living here."

The Burns journey brings to memory the time when Ian handled one of the Kilmarnock editions of the poems. I had long tried to fix a meeting between Ian and Sir Louis Sterling because, for one thing, Sir Louis had, in his Avenue Road house, a library of first editions worth £200,000, which is being gifted to London University. But—even bigger reason—Sir Louis started life in the same poor way as Ian—he sold newspapers on the East Side in New York—and I thought it would be really great to bring the two together.

One time, having failed to effect a meeting—the Sterlings were on holiday—Ian and I got into the library. He did not seem impressed when I told him that an edition of the Bible had cost £1,250; he paid more attention to the Shakespearian folios. But when the Kilmarnock edition of Burns was placed in his hands he sat down in silence for a few moments. Then he said, "Coming into this library takes me back to the first time I went into a house where there was a case full of books. It was on Wick's spring holiday, and I had borrowed a cycle for a run to Thurso. But the wind and the rain were against me, and I only managed to get as far as Castletown (five miles from Thurso). I went into Manson's Hotel and up the stairs. Before me was a bookcase, crammed full, and I sat on the floor and in time I had all the books around me. A woman came in and asked who had let me take out the books. I said, 'Nobody, but I couldn't resist putting my hands on them.' She looked at me curiously and then said, 'Maybe you can't resist putting your hand to a plate of broth?' I smiled and thus had food for the mind and body."

Ian asked me, "How much did Sir Louis pay for this edition?"

"Eight hundred pounds."

"Dear me," said Ian, "and Robbie Burns died in poverty,

persecuted by the Holy Willies who are a curse of every generation." Then he paused, and as he handed over the edition I heard Burns' words from his lips, "Man's inhumanity to man makes countless thousands mourn."

But he never met his brother Socialist, Sir Louis Sterling.

For years I had known Bart Kennedy, tramp, oyster fisher, opera singer, and friend of Lord Northcliffe when the Press peer was plain Alfred Harmsworth. Bart came of Irish descent from the Liverpool docks, and his early days were perhaps more painful than Ian's. His writing had a style of his own; he could sketch a pen picture with the fewest words I have ever known. Staccato English, but virile. He used to come to my office to hand over his thoughts on music, which were published by a music committee for propaganda purposes. And he could rise to wonderful heights in his flights of fancy.

Ian and he met one afternoon, and I can still see Bart staring at him from beneath those bushy eyebrows which stood straight out and saying to Ian, "Well, laddie, you're starting to write. Never use a big word where a little one will do. Write the best English. Like the Bible. Or mine."

"Like yours! You drop words," Ian told him.

"Drop words? Yes. But they fit where I want them, and readers never have their brains in a maze by any involved sentences or mile-long words of mine."

In a chat years afterwards Ian told me he had never forgotten Bart Kennedy or the nutshell advice handed out by him.

"We come the same way, and go the same way," was one of Ian's sayings about life. Equality and fraternity were words which came often to his lips in the time he spent with me.

There was a time when the late Alex James of the Arsenal, and Peggy, his wife, had lunch with me at the Café Royal;

and the three of us were standing at the bottom of the stairs when I saw Mark Hambourg coming down.

"Mr. Hambourg," said I, "allow me to introduce you to another great artist, Wee Alex James of the Arsenal. You've got it in the hands; he's got it in the feet!"

"So have I," returned Mark; "rheumatism."

Immediately afterwards I met Ian, who had been at a function in the same restaurant. "Quite true, what you said," he commented. "The same artistic impulses which flowed to Hambourg's hands went to Alex's feet, and Alex could produce as much magic with a football as any pianist could on a keyboard. We are all professionals, doing that which Nature intended we should do. This class distinction about a man's job is just sheer bloody nonsense."

Restless Ian remained to the end, and just as he paced up and down a newsagent's shop in Wick as a boy, so did he across my office—talking and thinking. I have the same habit myself, and there we would be, like a pair of caged animals walking across the floor, in different directions, until our heat subsided.

At that time I was re-reading *The Age of Reason*, by Thomas Paine, and Ian was reading it. We were argumentative about the beginning of the world, and because he thought I had put one point beyond him, he turned at me with heat in his voice:

"Can *you* tell me who created the Creator?"

I could make no reply, so said nothing.

He cooled down. "That's just it. No one knows the beginning of things; no one knows the end. And the basis of any religion, of all religions, should be, try to be honest, try to be kind." More than thirty years ago, yet I can hear his voice now.

The day came when the young Harmsworths, Harold and Bobby, returned to my office, and, after a chat, an arrangement was made whereby Ian Mackay joined the *Western*

Morning News, getting his first full-time employment in journalism.

In the after years we knocked against each other frequently, and for some time before his death we became again the friends we were in the 'twenties.

I persuaded him to come home to Wick for a visit when the "A Matter of Opinion" broadcasts were restarted. Then one evening in May 1952 Mrs. Mackay and he came with me to the Café Royal, and we lingered long over old times. Going up Regent Street, Ian and I talked of Little Titchfield Street days. He wanted to know what had happened to all the people who came up the first-floor stairs. Thus went our talk until we reached Hanover Square, and with the parting handshake there was the promise of a family lunch party when my wife and I came to London in September.

We came to London in September, but there was no lunch because we both had many engagements.

And then those stunning words in the calm of an early October evening: "Ian Mackay is dead."

The Student Adventurer

BY

CHARLES SUTTON

Charles Sutton, ex-foreign editor of the "Daily Express" and Industrial Correspondent of the "Daily Mail," is now a business executive on the "Daily Mail."

IAN MACKAY had a remarkable capacity for being where something unusual was happening or about to happen. It was as if adventure marched a few yards ahead of him beckoning him into a world of fantasy. Thus it was no wonder that on a certain day in 1920 when a young student of London University was contemplating an end-it-all dive from Waterloo Bridge, Mackay should arrive in time to stop him.

It was a warm spring day, and Mackay was enjoying one of his afternoons of truancy from University College. For no reason at all he sauntered from Gower Street in the direction of Waterloo Bridge, although it is pretty certain he went by way of Charing Cross Road, where he spent many of his student days rummaging through the second-hand book-shops. It did not seem remarkable to him that he arrived at Waterloo Bridge just as his fellow-student from University College was about to perish with his sorrows in the Thames. As he said afterwards, it was a happy encounter because it gave him an excuse for several days of truancy. He took the would-be suicide to his lodgings and gave him a robust introduction to the joys of hedonistic living.

The Mackay philosophy was already in those early student days beginning to take shape. He was piecing it together from chorus girls, barmaids, coffee-stall customers,

cabmen and the ardent, but shabby, intellectuals of Bloomsbury, as well as from professors of English literature,
political history and philosophy in Gower Street.

The first person to benefit from the Mackay theory of a
free and unrestricted life was the young man who nearly
went over Waterloo Bridge. He quickly cast away all care
and pursued pleasure almost with the same unbounded zest
of Mackay himself.

The second beneficiary, if my memory serves me loyally,
was a young woman who had been despoiled and abandoned
by another fellow-student. Mackay took over this situation
and spent all his money on steering the girl through her
troubles. Restored to health, she set out to face the world
fortified by a new courage, but she left behind a Mackay
sadly depleted of material wealth. After all you cannot do
much for a woman in trouble and keep yourself in any kind
of comfort on a Government grant of £3 a week!

It must have been about this time that Ian gladly accepted
pieces of left-off clothing. At times he was a sartorial com-
posite of his best friends. I have even known him wear one
man's trousers and another man's braces, and it was
commonplace to see him in odd socks.

Mackay blew into University College in 1919 like a wild
wind from the North of Scotland. He was soon recognised
as the leader of unorthodox and unconventional movements,
and he was a sturdy battle leader in a number of rags
between 1919 and 1921 which were distinguished by their
violence.

I was with him the night we captured "Pussyfoot"
Johnson, the American prohibition leader, whose hope was
to extend to Britain the dreary triumph he had enjoyed in
the United States. Mackay regarded compulsory temperance
as being only one degree better than enforced celibacy, so it
was natural that he should be one of the ringleaders of

this vigorous protest against an attempt to make Britain dry.

On the night of the rag, Ian, the light of battle flaming in his wild eyes, stalked into the Essex Hall in the Strand and demanded that Johnson cut out his lecture and take part in a debate—with Mackay. The prohibitionist would not be drawn, so Mackay and a number of chosen students, all ex-servicemen, seized him and carried him struggling from Essex Hall to King's College.

Here he was planted on a balcony and invited to drink a bottle of whisky. The man who had arranged the whisky was, of course, Mackay. "Pussyfoot" Johnson, who behaved with considerable dignity that evening, fought physically against the contamination of whisky, so he was hoisted on a stretcher and carried through the West End by hundreds of roaring students.

The evening ended unhappily for everyone, for in a skirmish between the police and the students "Pussyfoot" Johnson lost an eye. One of the most distressed people was the wild Mackay, who went off to hospital the next morning to condole with the injured man.

The ex-Black Watch private from Wick was indeed a turbulent character in those days. He was always searching for injustices. The more he could collect the happier he was, and he would fight like a leopard to get them righted.

I shall always have a picture in my memory of his tall, gaunt figure—as it then was—marching down Tottenham Court Road in front of a stolen gun, wildly waving a human shin-bone which he had seized from an invaded museum at Barts Hospital. His mane of untamed hair and open mouth, from which issued animal-like roars, gave him a terrifying appearance.

Ian was righting an injustice! It may not have seemed important to him in later years that Barts Hospital had been presented with a captured German field gun which they had proudly set up in their forecourt, and that University College had not been similarly honoured. But in those days it was a monstrous injustice and it provided Mackay with an opportunity to strike a blow against privilege. He was one of the leaders of a University College army which marched to Barts and stole their trophy.

One week in every month Mackay went pub-crawling. He knew all the famous ones in the West End, in Chelsea, in Brixton, in the East End of London, and it was in those student days that he laid the foundation of his incomparable knowledge of London pubs and music halls.

For the other three weeks in each month he went in search of knowledge and injustice, because his monthly allowance from the Government was practically exhausted in a week, and he was unable to indulge his love of romance until the next payment was due.

Those of us who lived with him in the Shakespeare hut, a students' hostel on a piece of waste ground in Gower Street, were kept awake at night listening to his tirades against the Black and Tans in Ireland and the maldistribution of wealth in England—the latter was his favourite subject because, as he said to me sadly many years later, "We had everything then—health, vigour, a feeling for romance, adventure— everything except money. Now the money is coming our way the vigour is evaporating."

But he couldn't really complain, for if ever a man set out to lead a full life and succeeded, it was this lovable giant.

Walter Duranty
and Ian MacKay
in Fleet Street

Ivan Opffer
New York 1953–

And so on—none of it being calculated to evoke such a chorus of appreciation from the Nonconformists and the Die-hard Tories of the West of England as would set up a clamour throughout the land for the services of the writer.

There were many, of course, who did admire his work, and not least among them politicians who could take a joke against themselves. But Fleet Street editors, if they read his early articles at all, ignored them. If Ian Mackay's career does nothing more than prove the fallibility of journalistic talent-spotters and encourage writers with talent to keep on keeping on until they are spotted, it will have done much for newspaperdom.

Yet his "comic cuts" was a mere relaxation. For several weeks before I took over from him I held a watching brief at the House. Mainly this meant following Ian around. I had written to him from Plymouth asking him to recommend a few books from which I could gather something of the background to the job. "Don't bother about books yet," he replied. "It's people that matter."

And so he spent those weeks introducing me to his friends. They ranged from Cabinet Ministers to Whips' messengers, from leader writers to copy boys. Constantly I was the stranger in his circle; yet magically the aura of good companionship which radiated from him made me feel one with his oldest acquaintances.

On Thursday nights, after getting off his news copy, he would sit down with a pencil and pad in the old Press Gallery Long Room—now converted into the dining-room—and say, "Now for some fun." After scribbling a paragraph or two, he would walk along the corridor to the cosy bar—now, alas, displaced by a chromium-plated cafeteria—and try out the jokes on the assembled company. Ideas were exchanged with the whiskies, and presently back he would go to dash off a few more bubbly pars.

I must not leave the impression that his attitude to the land of Trelawny, Drake and Blake was habitually flippant. Having lived for eighteen years in the West Country, I was amazed at the wealth of knowledge this man from the far north of Scotland possessed about the far west of England.

The secret was that he took every opportunity that came his way to study what he was writing about. General elections saw him roaming from Somerset to the Isles of Scilly in search of news and views, talking, talking, talking, learning, learning, learning.

Naval matters were of first importance to the *Western Morning News*. Accordingly Ian used to fix himself a passage with the autumn cruise of the Fleet when the House was up. He became equally at home on the spotless quarter-deck of a battleship and in the mire of a country cattle market. When questions were raised in the House about Cornish tin, china clay, or Brixham fishermen, he was as well informed as the experts.

He was not slow to acknowledge the value of his West Country experience. Knowing his humble origin, of which he made no secret, I asked him one day over a Scotch, "I suppose when you write your autobiography, Ian, you will call it, 'From log cabin to White Horse'." With that laugh which used to shoot his eyebrows almost up to the roots of his bushy hair he returned, "Not bad, Carlos. But no—it will probably just be, 'From John o'Groats to Land's End'."

Ian in the Lobby

BY

HARRY BOARDMAN

Harry Boardman is the parliamentary reporter of the "Manchester Guardian."

IAN MACKAY was but twenty-four when he entered the Lobby as Political Correspondent of the *Western Morning News* in 1922. This is a very early age to be taking up political journalism in the House of Commons, though let us not forget that still younger entrant to the Press Gallery, name of Charles Dickens. For eleven years Ian served the Plymouth paper at Westminster, so that he was thirty-five when he departed to join the *News Chronicle* and become, first, its Industrial Correspondent, and later the exuberant "columnist." (God forgive Fleet Street for taking over this Americanism.)

His development into the *News Chronicle's* winning writer on everything and nothing was no surprise to his former intimates in the Press Gallery. One of them, the late Herbert Sidebotham, who died before Ian's translation, would have thought the evolution natural if not inevitable. Sidebotham shone a very Sirius in the constellation of parliamentary journalists of those days. Everybody felt his superiority of mind and attainments (he had carried off the three great Oxford classical prizes) and everybody loved him for his modesty. He pronounced Ian one of the best conversationalists he had ever met and one of the most widely read men who had come his way. It was a judgment rich with promise.

By this time Ian was about thirty. He was drawn into the

circle that revolved around Sidebotham, the brilliant political journalist and humanist. Ian himself had something of the humanist temper. It was a secular humanism in which the Shorter Catechism played no part, but nevertheless few retained more of the Christian virtues of charity and unselfishness. As he matured during his eleven years he became a prodigal helper of newcomers and would as soon share a "scoop" with them as a yarn. He was ever the good companion. He carried about with him a Bohemian aura, if by Bohemianism is understood an indifference to convention and a love of good talk in a convivial atmosphere.

It was a Bohemianism worlds removed from the devil-may-care Bohemianism of an earlier Fleet Street day. It was the compensating side of a very industrious life, for Ian was a great worker and threw his whole being into his writing, while he was known to read half through the night and sometimes until the dawn. In short, he was one of those happily constituted beings who easily strike the point of balance between an active intellectual life and social pleasures, and the Press Gallery and the Lobby of the House of Commons can minister as, perhaps, no other place to such souls.

A Socialist himself, he found many of his friends in the Labour Party, but he had them also among the Tories and Liberals, and not least among the obscurer folk who keep the Palace of Westminster running. Of these must not be forgotten Rose and Annie, who, in their famous bars, have attended, for more than a generation, to the lubrication of Members' throats with tea and not-tea.

Ian had the humorist's faculty for seeing himself with amused detachment. He would tell of one of his first Lobby lessons in discretion. On a quiet night he was talking with one of his "locals"—the Lobby man's name for a Member from the region his paper serves. At the same moment another Member crossed the Lobby with his wife.

"Where, in the name of Heaven, did he pick up that frump?" demanded Ian of his "local," indicating the wife. "I would have you know, Mr. Mackay," answered the "local," "that that frump is my sister."

"Collapse of stout party," Ian would cry as he crumpled up with laughter in telling the story.

He had as a fellow-contributor to the *Western Morning News* R. J. Dingle, the wittiest and most cultivated of men, who still scintillates in the Press Gallery. Said Ian to him one day, "Dingle, you are doing a fine Christian work." "Oh," remarked Dingle with a speculative smile. "Yes," went on Ian. "They want to sack George Blank, but they daren't; he's the only man in the office who can read your handwriting."

Certainly, a fount of gaiety, wit and good fellowship was withdrawn from the Press Gallery when Ian departed.

"Merchant of Light"

BY

HERBERT TRACEY

Herbert Tracey, former journalist who joined the staff of the Trades Union Congress as Press Officer a generation ago, became accepted by Fleet Street as "The Voice of the TUC." Is a prolific writer on trade union affairs and personalities.

AMONG the Brethren of Salamon's House (in Bacon's *New Atlantis*) were some who were set apart to sail into far countries to "maintain a Trade, not for gold, silver or jewels, nor for silks, nor for spices; nor for any other commodity of matter, but only for God's first Creature which was Light: to have *light* (I say) of the growth of all parts of the world." And these adventurers were called "Merchants of Light."

Ian was one of the Brethren, and this was his Trade. His entry into any company where I was one, when we perceived his presence and even before he spoke, always seemed to me to have a *quickening* effect: he brought things to life. There was a radiation of energy, generated in the inner furnace of his being, an intensity of power, converted not into heat, but into a white-hot incandescence like a tungsten filament, or the mercury vapour lit by the electrical current.

Then we knew Ian had come amongst us, and we all began to brighten up, each of us feeling (as J. M. Barrie put it) that one could say a neat thing oneself too, if one were given time. It made no difference if one were in his company with others, or alone with him; the result was the same in all circumstances: his mind flashed and scintillated with the same dazzling effect for one as for many; and as Light was his merchandise he squandered it as prodigally as the spendthrift sun.

My first meeting with Ian—which could easily have been the last but for his good nature and entire absence of guile—revealed his quality. He had just taken over as Industrial Correspondent of the *News Chronicle*; it was the year (1934) which had been appropriated by the T.U.C. to celebrate the centenary of the Tolpuddle Martyrs. And I suppose that I was feeling a bit above myself as an officer of the T.U.C. in that (to us) exciting year. Moreover, I was working rather hard at the time, which might have excused, but did not justify, my petulance. At any rate I expressed displeasure over a minor inaccuracy in one of Ian's early news stories about the T.U.C., when—in the pompous phrase that suited my mood at the moment—my attention was drawn to it.

It was a very small point. He had written about a recommendation of one of the T.U.C. General Council's sub-committees as if it were a decision of the General Council itself, which had not yet considered it. The matter was of trivial interest, but when Ian was told that I'd placed him among Byron's *English Bards and Scottish Reviewers*, as one "with just enough of learning to misquote," his reaction was characteristic. He came down to Transport House to see me.

I remember my delight in gazing upon the wild Highlander (so I thought of him) for the first time. I believe we did not either of us refer to the error in his news story, after he offered me, at the very beginning, Samuel Johnson's explanation to the lady who asked him why he defined "pastern" as the "knee" of a horse.

Ian had no reason at all, of course, to plead ignorance of even such a minute detail about the mechanism of the

T.U.C. It was just a slip of the pen. Then, and afterwards, he impressed one with his really astonishing knowledge of the Labour movement, and its leading personalities—especially its personalities.

He went down to the Congress at Weymouth in that year and instantly found an assured place, not only at the Press table, but with kindred spirits among the delegates and members of the General Council; and he held that place at Labour assemblies literally until the day of his death.

It was at the Weymouth Congress, incidentally, that I had my one and only squabble with Ernest Bevin, on account of a service Ian Mackay rendered to us in the Tolpuddle Martyrs' Commemoration. He invited me to obtain an article for his paper from the Congress President of that year—the late Andy Conley.

Bevin was a little annoyed with me for my share in helping Ian to secure the article from Andy for a rival newspaper, at the height of the commemoration. Bevin reproached me for not getting Conley's article rather for the *Daily Herald* than the *News Chronicle*. We had "a few words" about it. But Ian exercised his charm upon all three of us—Bevin, Conley and myself; and the incident passed off, leaving no trace of resentment in our relationships.

It was during these centenary celebrations that I learned to appreciate Ian's abilities as a reporter dealing with trade union and Labour affairs. In his unhurried, casual way he followed every incident in the week's programme. One met him all about the place, and in every sort of company. He even followed me (I remember) to the N.C.L.C. Summer School which was held that year somewhere in Dorsetshire, to listen to what he described in print as my "brilliant" lectures: the only occasion I can remember of Ian's intentional misuse of the English language.

There was one feature of the Tolpuddle Commemoration which threw Ian into an ecstasy of delight. There was a great turn-out of the union delegations with their banners and emblems. They were marshalled in their procession to the amphitheatre outside the Tolpuddle village; and as they formed themselves in a great semi-circle around the platforms, the union banners blazed in the sun with the effect of a medieval pageant. The spectacle touched Ian's sense of history. It bore comparison (he said) with the Field of the Cloth of Gold, and had as much significance for him in the unfolding of our rough island's story.

There was not much in Ian's practice of his profession as an industrial correspondent to call forth his singular powers of imagination and memory. His news stories relating to our movement's affairs he collected at first hand in visits to Transport House, and the Government departments involved in them; and these writings of his were invariably well-informed and accurate; but their matter was prosaic.

It was only when he was able, having set down the facts, to soar away into descriptions of the interplay of personalities and policies of the Labour movement that one became aware of the untapped wealth of his imaginative understanding of the human interests with which the trade union and labour movement is primarily concerned. This he was to pour forth lavishly later in his Diary and essays.

There were strong affinities between him and many of the movement's leaders. He was happier in their company than perhaps in any other, save the companionship of his fellow-newspapermen. He saw the Labour leaders without their haloes and public faces; they dropped their masks in his company, and behaved not as potent, grave and reverend senators, but as all boys together. When they relaxed and became their natural selves at the adjournment

of Congress (for example), Ian was a welcome addition
to the party.

One unforgettable picture in the mind's eye is of Ian
standing up with members of the General Council to sing
wordlessly but with appropriate gestures "The Song of
Sixpence" with the joyous swoop of hands and body when it
came to the "bloody great blackbirds." They "Saw the Old
Homestead" too, and sat "Under the Spreading Chestnut
Tree" with muted tongues but significant actions—and Ian
was always slightly behind the other performers in suiting
the action to the unuttered words.

Yet it is not of Ian in these carefree connections, at the
customary *Bierabends* that marked the course of Congress
week and the conferences of the Labour Party, that one
retains the strongest impression. In my first encounter with
him he carried an armful of books. There was rarely an
occasion afterwards when he was not similarly burdened.
Much of our talk, when official matters were disposed of, was
of books and writers.

I could not follow him all the way into the by-paths of
literature. It did happen once or twice when I could make
him envious of an acquisition for one's library that he
had not himself laid hands on for his. I picked up, in
a second-hand bookshop, a little two-volume edition
of Sterne's *Sentimental Journey*, with the improper
continuation by Evoenius. He coveted it, and I lent it to
him.

As one bookman to another I pay testimony to his
scrupulous honesty in returning the volumes to me after a
reasonable lapse of time. This is, if I may be equally honest,
more than I did with several volumes of like nature that he
lent to me. Neither can I qualify for the pardon that Charles
Lamb extended to another inveterate book borrower,
Coleridge, whose thefts Elia was willing to condone on

Coleridge's plea that a book belonged to a person in the ratio of appreciation.

When we were talking one day about the monstrous growth of our collections of books, I said it was a pity that we could not take them with us. "Not take them with us?" said Ian: "then *I'm* not going!"

Ian knew more about books that I could claim to know, and made better use of them. His writings sparkle and dance with the light his mind and memory reflected from the books he picked up. And what a mind and memory were his!

Over and over again in re-reading his collected pieces, one marvels at his extraordinary aptitude to link together the most diverse incidents, places or persons in a flash-back of memory—and presumably of research: as when he named a goodly array—he called it "a very queer crew"—of people who shared his birthday with him. It included Shakespeare, Cervantes, Turner, Hardy, Anson, Allenby, Lord Haw-Haw, Cripps, Simone Simon, Charlie Brooks of the Manchester Press Club, Ethelred II, the "Unready," and Shirley Temple. How on earth did his memory encompass that motley crowd in the accidental association with himself as having been born on the same day of the year, though a different year, of course?

Repeatedly, in his writings, Ian's memory brought persons, places and things into an illuminating conjunction of this kind. How did he do it? His was the pen of a ready writer, and one knows from the way he lived his life that he rarely sat down at a table littered with books of ready reference. Memory served his purposes in writing those pieces in which names and places and significant events were combined to weave the tapestry of his prose.

Ian was an extroverted personality in his professional work. He had his withdrawn moods. He was capable of sitting like the gentleman in Browning's *Epistle* "folding his

two hands to let them talk, watching the flies that buzzed";
but most of the time the exigencies of his profession compelled him to live more on the surface of things, to take
note of them and to write on the spur of occasion.

Had he been less of a hard-driven newspaperman, Ian had
the temperament and the inclination to watch the world
go by, to saunter at will, and to write against no deadline.
What Robert Browning said of the only poet he ever knew
might have been written of Ian:

> ". . . he stood and watched the cobbler at his trade,
> The man who slices lemons into drink,
> The coffee roasters' braziers, and the boys
> That volunteer to help him turn its winch.
> He glanced o'er books on stalls with half an eye
> And fly-leaf ballads on the vendors' string
> And broad-edged bold-print posters on the wall.
> He took such cognisance of men and things,
> If any beat a horse, you felt he saw;
> If any cursed a woman, he took note;
> Yet stared at nobody—they stared at him,
> And found, less to their pleasure than surprise,
> He seemed to know them and expect as much . . ."

In writing of Ian in such happy circumstances a contemporary poet might not have been able to go on and deny
the legend that if you tracked him to his home—

> "You found he ate his supper in a room
> Blazing with lights, four Titians on the wall,
> And twenty naked girls to change his plate!
> Poor man, he lived another kind of life . . ."

For Ian, whatever the circumstances of his life or the
pressure of his work, had a genius for friendship. No man I
ever knew seemed to get so easily and quickly on a basis of

affection and comradely understanding with both men and women, and impart to them in full measure his own love of life.

And the end came to this Merchant of Light as I am sure he would have wished it to come: not with a long decline and a dimming of his faculties, but in a blaze of his own igniting at the Labour Party Conference in Morecambe in 1952.

The Man Who Couldn't be a Bore

BY

HUGH CHEVINS

*Hugh Chevins is chief Industrial Correspondent of the "Daily Telegraph"
and a former chairman of the Industrial Correspondents' Group.*

I T was late one night in the summer of 1937 in the rue
Daunou. A shower of one-franc pieces, flung from the
other side of the street, fell at my feet. They came from a
tall, angular, grinning figure, with coat-tails blowing and
pinwire hair standing out at all angles. "And where might
you be going, you black-hearted bastard?" was being
bellowed at me.

It was, of course, John Cockburn Mackay. One was not
surprised at the chance meeting. One was never surprised
at running into him in the oddest places and at the oddest
times.

I had gone to Paris for a few days for the Exhibition and
was taking a stroll after my wife and daughter had retired.
"Let's go to Harry's Bar and hear the boy on the piano for
an hour or two," said Ian. He was equally an authority on
Beethoven and swing. I declined. The invitation meant a
night on the tiles and I was *en famille*. So we agreed to meet
next morning. We parted, I to my hotel, Ian, as I learned
later, to an all-night round of the Left Bank haunts.

In the morning, he arrived at the hotel, bent on a day in
the amusement park at the Exhibition with my eleven-
year-old daughter. He could have spent the day at the

Louvre, or pottering around the bookstalls, or in more erotic pursuits in Montparnasse. He had catholic tastes and inclinations. But he was determined to act as uncle to a child for a day.

What a joyous time it was. The roystering boulevardier, with a gentleness that could have been saintly and with boundless extravagance, escorted Barbara, hand in hand, on a crazy tour of the franc-catching attractions. He stuffed her with ice cream and lemonade. He never flagged. At the end of the exhausting day he shook hands with the dignity of a courtier and left us. He was the leader of wild revelry in the Pigalle district later that night. That was Ian Mackay.

Once we were attending a Socialist International conference in Antwerp. In the early hours of one morning we quarrelled. It was a frightful row over a trifle—we never fell out over things that mattered. He berated me in a voice that thundered over the docks and gave vent to his illimitable vocabulary. Arms beating the air, he turned on his heel and stormed back to the hotel, vowing never to speak to me again. I followed.

At the hotel we occupied adjoining rooms with a communicating door. In the morning I was awakened by Ian, hair awry, pyjamas undone, roaring, "Wake up, Chevinsky!" He called in a waiter who was wheeling a wagon bearing the finest breakfast the hotel could provide. I remember it included melon and delicious ham, which were not easy to come by in those early days after the war. That, too, was Ian Mackay.

From Brighton to Blackpool, from Copenhagen to Rome, we did the rounds together in pursuit of news, mainly about labour. We sat side by side with kindred spirits like Trevor Evans, Frank Machin and Charlie Brooks at Press tables at countless conferences. We travelled by road, rail, sea and air on innumerable journeys. We lobbied Transport

House and trade union headquarters all over the country. We spent holidays together.

He embarrassed me, he abused me, he flattered me; never, for a moment, did his companionship bore me; never was there the faintest trace of meanness in any act of his. Whether he was in gay or serious mood, quoting McGonagall or Shakespeare, discussing relativity or telling Rabelaisian stories, it was always a stimulating experience to be with him.

One of the joys and privileges of one's life was to be present at the Thursday morning meetings at the Cheshire Cheese between Ian and Tommy Earp, as their conversation took in Sherlock Holmes, Babeuf, Bradlaugh, Stendhal, the great criminal trials, the arts and a myriad of other topics, obscure and surprising. John Leslie Randall sometimes put them, and particularly Ian, right in fact.

In an indefinable way he had the capacity to do and say the most outré things and publicly tear convention to pieces without outraging, annoying or harming anyone. No one but Ian could have asked the Salvation Army lass who hawked the *War Cry* every Friday night in Fleet Street, "Have you got your red flannel knickers on tonight, dear?" and not caused offence. The brave, smiling lass understood him as well as most of us. She administered a gentle homily before she sold the agnostic her paper. They invariably shook hands, Ian patted her on the shoulder, and they parted staunch friends.

Another warm friend of Ian's was little Kitty, the flower-girl, who carried her basket round the Fleet Street pubs nightly throughout the blitz. He, more than anybody, recognised the stout heart which beat beneath Kitty's homely exterior, but he never told her she was a heroine. Instead, he chivvied her about her apocryphal misdeeds, charged her with profiteering, said her flowers were already dead. He knew what he was doing; so did Kitty. She went on her rounds all the more bravely for having met him.

It was one of the colourful sights of Fleet Street when Ian met Prince Monolulu, the tipster, whose real name is also Mackay. Ian, so far as I know, never wagered a shilling in his life, but he discussed racing with his befeathered and berobed friend with the authority of an expert. Arms a-waving, plumes and hair a-blowing, the pair of them would roar at each other the latest titbits of racecourse gossip and then part, shouting mutually ribald farewells.

Perhaps there was a trace of exhibitionism in his ebullience, but I prefer to think it was an all-consuming zest for life and work which moved him along his unconventional path. Sometimes, he appeared a little dogmatic; I prefer to think that was conviction. Occasionally, he raged; but only against an injustice, a wrong done to a colleague.

Now and again his embroidery of an incident, in which his colleagues had figured, and recounted in their presence, was disconcerting.

For instance, when a crowd of us were seated in an hotel lounge after a day's work he would whip out his national registration identity card and say to me, "Show yours as well, Chev." I produced mine. "Now note the numbers," he would remark to the company. The numbers ran consecutively—AAAY/44/1 and AAAY/44/2. "Isn't that a fantastic coincidence—a chance in millions?" he asked. I could have given the simple explanation that we registered together when we were living in the same flat in Crane Court at the start of the war.

It was perhaps at that period that Ian lived his life at its most hectic, when he really turned night into day. His routine (a word he would abhor) when in London was something like this: Rise at 1 p.m., take lunch and read the newspapers; sally forth to Fleet Street pubs and clubs and engage his friends in conversation about the news of the day; reach his office somewhere in mid-afternoon and do his work in his own unique way; then, in the evening, seek out his friends in the pubs and clubs once again and for hours discuss, with astonishing expertise, any topic which arose.

When his colleagues, because of the lateness of the hour, reluctantly left him to go to their suburban homes, he sought other company in a club that remained open most of the night. When the club closed, his unquenchable zest took him to the market places of refreshment which enjoy special licensed hours.

Eventually, often around 7 a.m. or 8 a.m., he returned to the flat as I was rising, and gravely remonstrated with me for going to bed at respectable hours. He read a poem or two in bed and was soon asleep. For a long time it was his claim that he never went to bed on the day he got up. It was a claim that was justified.

Towards the end he mellowed and broadened. He became less rumbustious and cared more for the quiet pleasures of home life. He spent many hours among his beloved books. He was less careless about his appearance. He tamed his hair. But he remained the same loyal, lovable, learned, great-hearted comrade.

Portrait of a Reporter

BY

FRANK MACHIN

*Frank Machin, for many years Northern Industrial Correspondent of
the "Daily Herald," is now editor of its Northern edition.*

IN one of his stories O. Henry has a character who says
of another: "He asked me about nine hundred questions
. . . I know he's on a paper. . . . You see a man about
half shabby, with an eye like a gimlet, smoking cut plug,
with dandruff on his coat collar and knowing more than
J. P. Morgan and Shakespeare put together—if that ain't a
reporter I never saw one."

There you have Mackay, except for the cut plug: he gave
up smoking long before a duodenal ulcer brought him
treacherously close to teetotalism.

Mackay was a reporter. I can still see Ernest Bevin
elbowing his way through the throng at a swagger hotel,
brushing off a duchess or two on the way, to slap Mackay
on the back and say, "Hello, Iron." That venture in metal-
lurgy, in its popular pronunciation, was the nearest Ernie
ever got to mastering Mackay's Christian name.

But Ian provided Bevin with a joke he never forgot. The
then Minister of Labour launched an appeal for wives,
sisters and sweethearts to go into the war factories. Mackay
opened his report with the simple words: "Bevin wants
100,000 women." Bevin chuckled about it till his end.

Mackay was a good reporter, not so much because he
asked questions—although he could ask plenty, and what is
more remember the answers—but because he didn't often
need to. People naturally told him things, for the record as

well as off it. With him a confidence was inviolate. But he
was no arid reporter of facts as such. He embellished them
with the colourful phrase.

Of course the secret of his reporting and afterwards of his
immense success as a columnist was his kaleidoscopic
memory. Only Hannen Swaffer's could equal it. Who cared
if a quotation was a word or two out, or if there were some
slight confusion of place and exaggeration of incident? The
heart of the matter was always there, principally because it
was the heart of the matter which interested Mackay, the
play of personality and policy and not just the dismal figures
and facts. (Damn it, I shall become as alliterative as Mackay
if I go on!)

He devoured print. Every station bookstall and every
branch library where they sold throw-outs was to him a
hunting ground. He emerged with armfuls of books. I am
for ever grateful for an introduction to two of them: *A Narrow
Street*, that warm picture of Parisian life, and the moving
record of the naval mutiny at the Nore about 150 years ago,
The Floating Republic. Mackay was nothing if not catholic
in his reading. He gave me one book about black magic
which he could have had back any time.

But that memory! "This street," he would say in a tour
of the Manchester suburbs, "is the street where Charlie
Peace shot a policeman," and, in West Hartlepool, "This is
the town which made a fool of itself because the natives
didn't recognise a monkey cast up from a shipwreck."
As a Northerner I leave to others his vast knowledge of
London. Much as he loved it I can remember him saying
gloomily when the bombs were dropping and the Londoners
around went on serenely with their drinks, "The trouble is
these bloody Cockneys are too dumb to know *when* to be
frightened."

He took it as a personal affront that once when he sought

a weekend's respite in a remote Derbyshire village a German raider chose to unload a shower of incendiaries on the place.

London claimed Mackay. We in the outer regions shared him. No need to inquire where to look when Mackay was around. In Newcastle one headed like a homing pigeon, as he did, for the Marble Bar (you would not find it under that name). At Hull you turned into the street known as the Land o'Green Ginger, knowing that Mackay could not possibly resist a place with a name like that. In Edinburgh it was the George.

His greatest recreation was promenading. Just strolling along the promenade. Not at these God-forsaken arty places, with ye olde worlde cottages and rapacious souvenir-sellers waiting for customers, but in the holiday places where the people crowded, where the barkers coaxed them into the sideshows and where the uninhibited masses in fancy hats paraded arm in arm. Mackay was not merely a democrat; he was of the democracy.

He was, besides, the greatest pavement-pounder I ever knew. In Plymouth he discoursed about the very stones we walked upon because they were marble. Together we walked the promenades from Brighton to Hove, from the Spa at Scarborough to the North Bay, from Douglas Head to Onchan Head in the Isle of Man and from Great Orme to Little Orme at Llandudno. Always talking. Mackay never stopped.

Yes he did. He once stood petrified whilst the barker outside a side-show, shouting the odds about the marvellous fortune-teller inside, related how the editor of the *News Chronicle* had sent for this king of all the star-gazers for information and advice. Mackay never tired of listening to that, any more than he did to the band which in an underground enclosure at another resort played the 1812 Overture with firework effects five times a day.

Ah, the talking, though! It ranged over everything. Whether William Wallace, the Scots whae hae man, was a Welshman. Would Nye Bevan ever be Prime Minister. Wasn't the original George Formby a better Lancashire comedian than his son ever knew how to be. Had D. H. Lawrence added much to literature. Did Willie Smith come from Durham or Yorkshire, according to where we were at the time, and wasn't Joe McCall from Preston the best-ever centre half-back. Or the talk might just as easily be about the law of diminishing returns.

Now and again even we were overcome by the beauty of our land, as when the setting sun mellowed the asperities of our longest stretch of concrete promenade. I said:

> "Sweet to ride at evening from the wells
> Where shadows pass gigantic on the sand,
> And softly through the silence beat the bells
> Along the golden road to Samarkand."

Mackay shouted, "*Forth*. 'Sweet to ride *forth* at evening from the wells.' " I conceded it. Naturally he countered with Shakespeare:

> "Turning with the splendour of his precious
> eye the meagre cloddy earth to glittering gold."

I said, "No *the*. 'Turning with splendour . . .' " Mackay was flummoxed.

But Mackay is now more likely to go a-roistering with Kit Marlowe than a Shakespeare pining for his Dark Lady. He will adventure with Verlaine rather than browse with Wordsworth. He will greet Keir Hardie respectfully, as befits a fellow-countryman, but will share his vision of a Merrier England with Robert Blatchford. Will Fyffe will be the one with whom he will exchange salty stories and he will pay court audaciously to Marie Lloyd.

Because time and place will matter not he will inveigle Jack Johnson and Jim Jeffries into the ring again, and at some celestial football match will have the mountainous form of Billy Foulkes in goal. His talk of newspaper days and sticky nights will be with old Freddie Chant rather than with C. P. Scott and the august editors of *The Times*. He will certainly settle finally the affair between Moriarty and Sherlock Holmes.

Come to think of it, I fancy he will be waiting to welcome *me*. He will meet me with outstretched hand and a gusty roar of, "Frankie, you black-hearted bastard. How's Whitney? How's Reg Butler? How's Charlie Brooks?"

How, he will demand, are all the newspapermen from one end of the country to the other—who will live in his memory as he lives in ours.

Ian and Palethorpe

RONALD WALKER

Ronald Walker, the Air Correspondent of the "News Chronicle," and
one of Fleet Street's brightest conversationalists.

W HEN I was young I had an aunt who was quite
a remarkable character. Let it be understood at
once that she had nothing to do with Ian Mackay.
She was unaware of his existence. The point is that she had
the misfortune to catch typhoid fever. Being a stalwart of the
Victorian age she emerged from the ordeal unbowed; but
from then on her life fell naturally for her into two parts.
As she got older the happenings in her long life were sign-
posted by this major event. This was Before Typhoid and
that was After Typhoid. B.T. and A.T.

For myself and others of his many friends, the Fleet Street
career of Mackay fell into two periods divided distinctly by
the duodenal trouble which developed in the late thirties.
It was known to Mackay's intimates as the Rat. It gnawed at
his innards more and more frequently until, to the astonish-
ment of all, he consented to consult a doctor.

This anonymous character, and character he must have
been, did what most others had never been able to do. He
frightened the life out of Mackay. He did it by the simple
process of explaining to Mackay that if he did not regulate
his life to some reasonable pattern he—the doctor—would
be obliged to slice up Mackay with a very sharp knife, cut
bits out and sew him up again.

The threat was the cause of transforming Mackay from the
shock-haired, pencil-thin, bedraggled figure into the smoothly

clothed aldermanic Mackay—who vanished so suddenly
that he remains with me yet, thundering the denunciations
that echo down the years of memory.

In the Before Duodenal age is founded the roots of the
reputation and fame of Mackay. The understanding commentator on his fellow-humans, the brilliant speaker, the
erudite essayist, were the flowerings of the B.D. period.
The B.D. Mackay had so much of the rude rumbustiousness
of the Elizabethan age, the age of Shakespeare and Marlowe.
With him died the last of the great characters of Fleet Street,
which produced a gallery of never-to-be-forgotten personalities through the years when there was room in the
newspaper world for character and temperament.

There is in the Press Club, among the collection of pewter
beer mugs, one which is inscribed with the name of "Ronald
Walker," and underneath, in brackets, the name "Palethorpe." The explanation gives an inadequate memoir of
the early Mackay.

It begins in the early 'thirties, when he joined the *News
Chronicle* as Industrial Correspondent. I had known him
before then, mostly in pubs, and almost always engaged in
violent, vociferous discussion, if not argument. Underneath
the unmanageable shock of wild hair was the lean face and
the beaked nose, topping the almost skeleton frame, always
rather inadequately clad in clothes which should have been
discarded long before. There were usually one or two essential
buttons missing, replaced by a bent safety pin which refused
to work any longer.

To such shortcomings Mackay was supremely oblivious.
He adored pubs, people and talking. The engulfing, dis-
integrating overcoat pockets would be stuffed with his
selection of current reading, which would include, bewilder-
ingly, Shakespeare, a cheap film magazine, Wisden's, a very
rude book indeed, and a translation of Plato.

His friends stayed to talk while Mackay thumped the counter and proclaimed and washed down his observations with copious swallows. Strangers gathered round to wonder at the decrepit-looking character who was the centre of the circle, and then found themselves fascinated by the charm, humanity and intellectual honesty which cut as cleanly as a surgeon's knife.

Somehow, we became companions. I still do not quite know how. Hair flying wild, coat weighed down by his portable library, he would drag me off into the night on pub crawls. We would walk miles from pub to pub, switching from street to lane and to alley as Mackay plotted the course, remembering that there was another just around the corner, or along the street. He would finish his glass at a gulp, bang it on the counter and shout to me, "Come on, you rat, into the night."

So we would sweep out, often from an astonished silence in the bar.

But often our arrival in a bar was so different. Mackay would stalk in and loom over the counter. At the far end a harassed barmaid would look around. Her face would break into a beam of welcome. Glasses, drinks, sandwiches, customers would be dropped. She would rush forward with a delighted cry of "Jock!"

Mackay would bellow some such endearment as, "Well, you old battleaxe," and then follow it up with the most intimate question regarding her very personal life. The response was a giggle and a remarkably frank answer. Mackay would boom in reply, "It is high time you did something about it."

All this in a startled hush among the nearby customers and to the disapproval of the manager. And then the manager would find himself caught up in a typical Mackay discussion, be it flat racing or the life of Frank Harris, to remain a friend always ready to welcome him.

These expeditions carried us over a wide field, from the East End to the West End, the spaces between, Bloomsbury and Holborn, and beyond to Chelsea and South London. Once embarked it was not possible to say where we might end up. The journey would be punctuated by the Mackay cry, "Come on, into the night."

One Saturday night Palethorpe was born, suddenly and without warning. We had arrived at a pub not far from Berkeley Square. Now Mayfair was not exactly a Mackay stamping ground. He wanted to go there because he remembered the pub before it was rebuilt, and, of course— for Mackay—ruined. There we were with no welcome and unknown.

Mackay became fascinated by a conversation between two quietly spoken men. It became obvious that they were two butlers discussing their staff problems and domestic difficulties. Politely Mr. Johnson asked Mr. Hutchins whether he would care for the other half. Mr. Hutchins said he would be obliged.

Listening to this conversation I was suddenly surprised to hear Mackay say in a loud voice, "Palethorpe, you may have the pleasure of buying the Master a drink." I spotted that he was gazing at an advertisement for Mr. Palethorpe's sausages, and I had the wit to say without pause, "Sir, I should be honoured."

That was the birth of Palethorpe. It silenced the bar, and we finished our drinks as the object of curious, puzzled glances from Mr. Johnson, Mr. Hutchins and all present.

From then on I was Palethorpe. He would sweep me into pubs and carry on the characters of master and butler with tremendous gusto. Listeners would be astonished by the most improbable conversation from the shock-headed Mackay.

They would hear him question Palethorpe as to the situation below stairs; whether the new parlourmaid, a buxom, toothsome piece, was behaving; he was sure the first footman was getting at the port; he trusted Palethorpe was not getting ideas above his station by being asked to drink with the Master.

You could see puzzled eyes taking in the long, lean figure, beginning with worn-out dancing pumps (goodness knows where they came from, but he did climb Mount Snowden in them), odd socks, the trousers with the safety pin, and the rest.

It was splendid fun, especially when Palethorpe was thunderously abused for being a snob, a reactionary, a Fascist beast and an ignorant wart on the base of humanity.

In those days Mackay lived in what he was pleased to call The Drain. He occupied one room on the ground floor of an old house, once the home of Keir Hardie, in Nevill's Court. This was one of a maze of narrow alleys which ran across an area to the immediate north of Fleet Street, behind the Cheshire Cheese and near Gough Square.

The house and, indeed, all of Nevill's Court disappeared in the bombing of London. All that is left is a large hole in the ground revealing decaying brick foundations and the remains of ancient cellars.

Not long before his death Mackay leaned against a wooden railing, surveyed the hole and said, "There it was. See, a tree has grown already underneath The Drain." And then he went on remembering in such vivid detail that it cannot be recorded here. Perhaps the tree will remember, and keep it all to itself.

The Drain was Mackay's citadel against the world. In those B.D. days he had little regard for creature comforts. He steered straight for fundamental essentials. The Drain had a bed, a cold linoleum floor, a mat, a round table, a chair, a wardrobe and a sordid sink. For light there was a gas burner that belonged to another age.

With the background of The Drain, Mackay claimed to be the only journalist who was a genuine resident of Fleet Street. From deafening sessions in the Press Club he would hurl a final denunciation at the bar in general and sweep down the stairs with the cry, "Back to The Drain."

Occasionally he would make the most preposterous statements. One he made often was that he had for years never gone west of Temple Bar. When Palethorpe ventured to mention that the Master had recently appeared at places far west, he would be greeted with a volley of abuse and told roundly to keep his place and mind his business.

Whether Mackay was a conscious builder of the Mackay Legend is difficult to say. It is still recalled that in those days Mackay never ate. He used to say so himself; but Palethorpe used to get into frightful trouble by pointing out that in the course of four or five pubs the Master had taken in without apparently noticing, two sausages, a plate of ham, a pie and yet another sausage.

A tree grows in Nevill's Court.

Ian the Ubiquitous

BY

JOHN MACADAM

*John Macadam, sports columnist and essayist, one of the best-known
personalities in Fleet Street, has served on many newspapers, including
the "Daily Express," and is now with the "Daily Sketch."*

WHEN we were helling around in the old days well
before the war, I infested an old glass-canopied
garret of a place just off Fleet Street, behind
Dr. Johnson's house in Gough Square. Local legend was that
it had once been a studio frequented by the pre-Raphaelites
and, in its more recent life, had been used as some sort of
sub-branch by the suffragettes at the height of their
campaign.

Be that as it may, it became a frequent, disturbing—and
very pleasant—habit for all sorts of kindred spirits to clamber
up those rickety old wooden stairs armed with bottles for the
purpose of making a night of it.

Many a night we did make of it and, looking back to those
who used to enjoy the singing, declaiming, arguing and,
occasionally, the scrapping, I reflect that Ian was most
closely in tune with whatever atmosphere still clung to the
old place.

My reading and occasional geographical surveys of the
surrounding streets had led me to believe that this was the
studio in which Swinburne would write an ode and then
dash into the street to declaim it to the night; in which
Sylvia Pankhurst strove for emancipation. Truly, it seems
to me, Ian had a dash of both of them for, despite all the
bonhomie and bookishness, he was large part poet and large
part fighter.

THE HAPPY WARRIOR

—by Bert Thomas.

Another thing about him was his acute everywhereness. I never consciously set off anywhere with him, but the number of odd corners of the capitals of Europe in which we encountered each other couldn't be counted on the fingers of a twelve-toed baboon.

No part of inner London was safe, of course, for he was a voracious inner-Londoner; but it could be disconcerting (however happy) to be making your way up the Hill in Paris or along the Ramblas in Barcelona and hear that same uncompromising voice demand, "Well, Johnny. How's the Morton getting on?" Greenock Morton was my home team.

The record in these *rencontres* was established once when I found myself head-to-head with him among a heap of tattered volumes in a Farringdon Street book barrow and then, at two o'clock the following morning, found him again in Harry's Bar in the rue Daunou in Paris, thundering McGonagall and insisting that the bewildered Negro piano player accompany him *softly*.

That was a great bond between us—our regard for these two great Dundee characters: the late poet and tragedian McGonagall and the very present Harry McElhone and his (in the words of dear old Sparrow Robertson) Thirst Emporium.

Strangers to Harry's place must often have wondered at us two foreigners, Ian with the way of an eagle and the little one with the large moustache, declaiming at each other mightily until the tears ran down our cheeks. What could they know of McGonagall who only Verlaine know?

Harry's greatest virtue, and he has many besides, is his calm acceptance of almost everything. You never surprised him any more than you would ever surprise Ian. Harry never sees anything incongruous about the college coats of arms with which he decorates his bar. Ian would stand below them, glass in hand, laying down the law on any subject that came up as if he were the Master of Pembroke in person. He always made his background his own; spiritually, a kind of chameleon.

He wasn't running his column in those days or he would surely have written the piece to end all pieces about Harry. As it was, I went on a sports story one time and did that thing myself . . . told the story of the little Dundonian who emigrated to the U.S.A., made himself first king of the cocktail shakers and came home at the outbreak of the first world war to join the army.

Harry was demobbed in 1918, settled in Paris, married a French wife and opened the bar he has since made one of the best known on both sides of the Atlantic. It has been all these years, and still is, a clearing-house for newspapermen from all over the world. Ian and I constantly crossed paths and destroyed many a thirst there.

One of those nights I recall more clearly than others. It was early in the recent war and I was in Paris on soccer business. My story had gone, and I was settled in on Harry's bar for the night when Ian stormed in with, apparently, the same high-minded intention.

He might have stepped straight out of Fleet Street for all the surprise he evinced; the buttoned-tight mackintosh and the couple of books he'd picked up from a barrow were as always. Harry's eldest son, Henri, on leave from the Maginot Line, was spending a last nostalgic night serving in the bar but, with the arrival of The Mackay, he was round with us.

As the night wore on, Ian noticed my tie—an Olympic souvenir from one of the Scottish team at Berlin—and when Ian spotted the old golden lion rampant of Scotland he loosed all his eloquence in McGonagall and finished up, "That tie rightly belongs to young Henri—the only Scots poilu in the Maginot Line!"

Henri looked very Scottish in my tie and Ian beamed as if

he had invented the Auld Alliance. As I recall it, he and I brought in the dawn up the Hill, perched precariously on high stools in a bistro eating eggs.

Others will tell about his memory. I can only testify to its fantastic quality in relation to sport. On those occasions when we met abroad, I would be on sporting business, he on politico-industrial, of course. But, whereas I had the haziest outline of the reasons for his conference, he would be full of questions about why this player was dropped in favour of that or would the English boy be fit at the weight for tomorrow's fight?

I introduced him on one Paris trip to Jeff Dickson and was careful to let Jeff know that Ian dealt with industry. Well, if there was one thing dear old Jeff wanted to have no part of, far less make polite conversation about, it was industry. I needn't have worried. Ian sailed straight into a very funny reminiscence of the first fight he saw in Wick and then plunged into boxing politics as if he did nothing else.

You had only to mention Glasgow Rangers and he would say, "What a half-back line . . . Young, Lonie and Hay." He would give you the entire Sunderland side of the same period—when he was quite a boy. I don't remember ever seeing him at a football match or a fight but he could talk with the historians about both and keep his end up.

One of his favourite McGonagall pieces was that dedicated to the Railway Bridge of the Silvery Tay, and when he ranted in the grandiose manner appropriate to the poet's works . . .

".. . With your numerous arches and pillars in so
        grand array,
    And your central girders, which seem to the eye
    To be almost towering to the sky . . ."

he might almost have been reciting his own epitaph.

A Few with Ian

BY

OLIVER ST. JOHN GOGARTY

*Oliver St. John Gogarty, former Senator of the Eireann Republic,
well-known Dublin doctor, wit and poet. Now lives in New York.*

HE said any time after midnight. Ian is a man of his
word, I thought; and there he was leaning against the
bar with his back turned. I would know that straight
back anywhere with its square, lean shoulders and its dark
brown coat. He was talking to someone. I couldn't see the
other fellow; but when I did see him he wasn't much anyway.
Ian nodded when he saw me: we were old friends.

He was holding forth on the presumption of jerry-builders
who called their houses and terraces by magniloquent names.
"I suppose in Gravesend you live on the Esplanade or in
Palace Mansions?" The little man emitted a hardly audible
sound. It meant that he was not offended though he did live
somewhere near Gravesend with his sister. Ian looked down
his twisted nose at the little man. He seemed surprised that
he had not been taken seriously.

I can't remember the little man saying, "Good night." He
slipped away unnoticed. Ian looked down at the empty
space. I ordered a tankard and eyed it carefully to see that
it had not my name engraved on it, for it is a rule of the
club that if you get your own tankard it is drinks all round
and on you. But the name on the pewter was "Mickey."
That meant Lord Killanin.

I read the name to Ian. Ian smiled reminiscently. "Did
you hear that after the King's coronation, Killanin drove

down in full regalia to the Cheshire Cheese and speared a sausage on his sword?"

Suddenly in came Paul Bewsher. Paul was radiating energy. Though he was below middle height you never noticed it. He never gave you time. Ian looked at him and ordered a double Scotch.

"Did you hear this one?" Paul asked.

> "Last night when I dined with the King
> He did a remarkable thing:
> When the turbot came on
> He . . ."

The little man came back. Another drink was ordered.

Paul shot another limerick at us to make up for the one that had been interrupted. Then he lifted his glass; gave one gulp and disappeared.

Ian said, "I have always wanted to meet the author of a limerick. For the thousands who repeat them, you never find one who composes them."

The little man spoke up. He must have gained courage from his visit elsewhere for he asked Ian with the respect one gives an oracle, "What is the best woman you have ever had?" Ian delivered the *pronunciamento*, "The best woman you ever had is your first. Then the woman you are living with at present." That seemed to satisfy the little man, who was, anyway, living with his sister.

"Talking of women," I said, "I hear that Wales has the highest rate of illegitimacy in the three kingdoms." "Nonsense," said Ian, "Scotland for ever!" "Wait a while," I said, "I saw old Lloyd George the other day on the terrace of the House and I asked him, 'Why are there no divorces in Wales?' 'No complaints,' was the immediate answer, which was not bad seeing that he expected me to talk politics in the House of Commons."

The little man went off in a huff. Ian looked after him and said, "I wouldn't have thought he was a Welshman."

When we had settled again, Ian asked, "Did you ever hear of the 'Ball at Kirriemuir'? No. Well, it is the most licentious poem in the language." I said, "It can't be worse than 'Luckie Spence's Last Advice,' by honest Alan Ramsay."

"Worse," said Ian. There's no accounting for the strange places that Apollo chooses to manifest his sacred strength. Glasgow of all places!

Dawn was breaking when I found myself by Ian's side as we walked past Ely Place. Before us the many spires of Christopher Wren were standing up in the white morning. It was a still and tranquil sight. "Earth has not anything to show more fair" was as far as I could go.

But Ian, whose thought was more devious, announced, "They have large ears, they have long feet, they have no fear, they live in secret but they are known to one another, and they cannot imagine defeat."

He was thinking about the governors of England to whom Kings and Prime Ministers are but walking shadows. They are the substance. They live in the past and the present and in the future; and they never get into the news.

Ian of the Warm Heart

HANNEN SWAFFER

Hannen Swaffer, "The Pope of Fleet Street" and a pioneer of popular journalism, has been editor of many newspapers, but won international fame as dramatic critic and columnist. Now writes for the "Daily Herald," "The People," and other Odham's publications.

IAN MACKAY, had he possessed ambition, might long since have been acknowledged as one of the most brilliant essayists of our generation. But he spent his time in loving his fellow-men, instead of climbing into a place above them.

He lavished his gifts, and his knowledge, in talk with those he met—his fellow-craftsmen among all parties, the trade unionists, famous and humble, whose work for human betterment he regarded as one of the greatest hopes of mankind, people he met in pubs, fellow-passengers in trains. To him, they were all the same—"people." Among my friends only George Lansbury and Will Rogers possessed, to the same extent, an equal disregard for importance or obscurity.

So it was not until 1945—when he was forty-seven!—that Mac was "discovered."

For years he had spent his working hours in one of the dullest* of occupations, being an industrial correspondent. Such a being only gets the headlines when there is a "strike" —usually a lock-out—and then days and days have to be spent watching the tragedy of idleness and hardship.

Then, one morning, I read in the *News Chronicle* the first of his vivid descriptions of the election contest which,

*Dullest? Not on your life, Mr. Swaffer!—Ed.

142

unknown to any of us, was to sweep Labour into a victory that led to the foundation of the Welfare State. Mac, at long last, had as a subject one not only dear to his heart, but one that was dramatic and eventful.

His were, indeed, the most brilliant articles penned during that historic election campaign. In a few weeks he made—after all the years of frustration and self-effacement—a great personal reputation.

Then, to his lasting credit, Gerald Barry gave Mac his head. And, from then until his death, the most talented of all Fleet Street's personal columnists was allowed to display to millions of delighted readers the surprising profundity of his literary knowledge, the aptness of his gift for analogy and quotation, and the wit and virtuosity of which, hitherto, he had revealed only in his conversation.

I remember particularly the emotional eloquence of Ian's obituary of Alexander Thompson (of the *Clarion*) and—in utter contrast—his fascinating account of a visit he paid to a bookshop in San Francisco. No one I ever knew could find such enthralling copy as he did among the back-seat delegates to a trade union conference. Such a gathering was, to him, not a series of resolutions or a counting of heads, but an occasion to study types in whom Dickens would have delighted.

Often, when reading him, I have said to myself, "I wish I had written that." I have been called, in my time, "a first-rate reporter." But, although I have, as Ian had, a lead pencil, I do not possess his eyes, or his never-failing sympathy of outlook.

Had he written books, he might have been another Charles Lamb or a less contrary Chesterton. Had he been a literary critic, he would have ranked among the most widely read of them all. Had he put into volumes some of the love he had for our incomparable London—the only world capital with a soul—generations unborn would have revelled in his pen-sketches of its by-ways and its courtyards and its shopping streets and its eternal, tolerant, broadminded, all-welcoming Cockneydom.

But, no, he died what he was all his adult life—just a journalist, a man who writes today what will be read tomorrow and used as wrapping-paper the morning after. Fleet Street immeasurably gained by that because it was enabled to enjoy a friendship that never wavered in its loyalty and an affection that hundreds of us will long treasure.

I first remember of Ian that he told me that he lived in Keir Hardie's flat. I recall his having said that every time I saw him. And, in some ways, he was like the Keir whom I honour beyond almost any man. Ian had Keir's Scottish stalwartness, his ability to see to the heart of things, his faith in his fellow-men.

It was not, however, until the evening that followed one of the bitterest days of my life that I got really near to the warm heart that was hidden by his uncouth, ill-kempt exterior. We were seated—David Keir, Ian and I—in the lounge of the Grand Hotel, Brighton, a few hours after Ernest Bevin, in the cruellest speech he ever made, had caused the expulsion of Lansbury from the leadership of the Labour Party. Everybody was quarrelling—the Rights and the Lefts heatedly threw angry words at each other.

Even when I ventured to remark, "Bevin need not have used such sneering words about Lansbury as he did," both the chairman of the Labour Party and the chairman of the T.U.C. said to me, "If you don't agree with that, get out of the Party!" Ian, who heard this, poured out consoling words. "The Labour Party has a soul that nothing can destroy," he said. "Individuals don't matter. Personalities don't count. Think of the cause, Swaff."

For, disgusted, I was actually thinking of leaving the movement. Ian, David and I talked far into the night, while the rows still went on. Ian was persuasive. David, a Liberal, listened long and patiently. And Bevin was still so full of anger three days after that when, not wishing to part on bad terms with a man who had done so much for the masses, I put my arm through his and said something placatory, he replied, "Whenever I see a martyr or a saint, I see a humbug!"

"Ernest," I said, "you've forgotten your own years of martyrdom."

But how right dear Ian was when, a week later, I addressed a Labour meeting at Ilford (or Leyton) and there were scenes of fervid enthusiasm. No one in the hall seemed to remember there had been such an awful row at the Party conference. Labour was still on the march.

Largely, it was because of the Ian Mackays and the Jim Middletons—he, too, could see only the best in people—that the heart of the Party was sound, and still is.

Fleet Street has lost, in Ian Mackay, one of its finest human beings. The world of letters has lost a wasted genius. And scores and scores of reporters like myself have lost what kindred spirits in another sphere will gain—a great friend.

Mackay Writes a Column

BY

RITCHIE CALDER

Ritchie Calder is the science editor of the "News Chronicle" and a frequent contributor to the "New Statesman." Has published many books on scientific and economic subjects.

NONE of his cell-mates ever really accepted the redoubtable Hughina. In the privacy of the special-writers' room (if any room which Mackay shared could ever be regarded as private) we maintained that his grannie never existed.

This he would vociferously refute. He claimed that he himself was biological proof of her existence because, while he flagrantly encouraged doubts about his immediate origins, one thing (he said) was certain: he was not a product of spontaneous generation. Furthermore, if the company was mixed, he would threaten to produce visible proof, her finger-prints, the stigmata of Hughina, on that part of his anatomy which he claimed she "skelped" every morning on the principle (justified no doubt by experience) that he would do something during the day to deserve it.

Presumably he did have a grandmother, who may have been quite a character in her own right, but Grannie, that sibyl of Wick, familiar to his readers, was largely synthetic. Even her geographical location varied. In 1934 he was writing, "With a stout pencil and a good pair of spectacles, my grandmother would have made a better job of it without leaving her armchair in the Hebrides." Each of his colleagues at one time or another was Ian's grannie because when he was short of copy he would start a philosophical argument and next morning one of us would find himself being quoted in terms of "As my old grannie used to say. . . ."

She, with some help from Socrates, or Shakespeare or Sherlock Holmes, was the *dea ex machina* who rescued Ian out of the predicament in which all good journalists are liable to find themselves an hour before dead-line—a blank sheet, a blank mind, and a blank space to be filled in a newspaper. Then he would invoke Hughina and she never failed him. Consider the possibilities of that opening gambit:

"My grandmother, whose conversation consisted almost entirely of epigrams and clichés, spiced with an occasional excerpt from Leviticus or the Book of Revelations, used to say . . ."

Mackay was in the true Grub Street tradition. He could never really write unless those galley-masters of the Muse, the sub-editors, were clamouring for his copy. That did not, by any means, imply that he started thinking about his column at teatime, because all the time he was thinking about it. His was a magpie mind, continually picking up information, hoarding the inconsequentials, tagging the tags and indexing men's idiosyncrasies.

But his was also a trained mind. He despised the dilettantes who drifted into Fleet Street, with the veneer of a college education and the assumption that journalism owed them a living, who looked upon life with a Regency disdain and thought that newspaper work was just coining chi-chi phrases. When he was not calling them something much worse, he referred to them as "The Go-and-See Boys" who could only describe things because they did not know what questions to ask on a door-step or how to find the right sources. He, on the contrary, had come up the hard way of the shrewd, fact-finding, hard-working reporter.

I knew a whole procession of Mackays, who added up to the Ian of later fame. The "John" of thirty years ago, who used to come peddling London letter pars to the Scottish paper on which I then was. He was then slim and tall, full of energy and persistence, with a lolloping gait, and, as I still insist against his own claim to be a Black Mackay, with a shock of red hair. (If he hadn't, he was the type that should have had.)

He was serious then and shy (the truth was he was always shy, even behind that rumbustious good fellowship of later years). Then there was "Mac," which meant that he had got a toe-hold into the cameraderie of Fleet Street. Then "Jock," sound on his parliamentary facts as House of Commons man of the *Western Morning News* and (as I knew him) standing in occasionally for Ernest Hunter as Lobby Correspondent of the *Daily Herald*. Then "Ianto," the glorious swashbuckler of that band of rough-riders, the industrial correspondents. Then "Ian Mackay, diarist."

There were intermediate incarnations in the *karma* of the Bouverie Street Buddha. There was, for instance, "Wun Fang Yan, the Toothless Terror of Tottenham." That was when Mackay, with characteristic perversity and in defiance both of his dentist and of appearances, clung resolutely to a solitary tooth which wobbled. He would boast, "I can still say that all my teeth are my own," and claim that he could eat anything with it—except lettuce. Ian could never look sinister, but he used to pretend that his one fang made him sinisterly attractive. Sometimes he would succeed in disconcerting a new tea-girl by baring his gums and his fang, leering at her and snarling, "Ar har, me proud beauty, yer maiden innocence shall not save you . . ."

Working in the same room with Mackay could never be dull but, heaven knows, it could be distracting. When I teamed up with him after the war, we worked in quarters as close as a submarine. Indeed, Ian had a scheme for installing a periscope so that we could be forewarned of depth-charges from the Directors' Floor! Crammed into the room were Ronald Walker, the Air Correspondent; Charles Fothergill, the Motoring Correspondent; Margaret Stewart, Ian's successor as Industrial Correspondent; Geoffrey Cox, the Lobby Correspondent, when the House was not sitting; Robert Waithman, in interludes as American Correspondent, and Maisie Rosenthal, our secretary.

But even when the others were all out, the room was still overcrowded by the presence of Ian—his leviathan sorties in search of reference books, his bellows of execration at this or that or them or his prodigious encounters with the telephone.

Ian on the telephone—that was something! Maisie had strict instructions never to admit he was there. She literally blushed at some of the lies he made her tell. "Say I'm in Birmingham," he would whisper and, when she had passed the message, he would suddenly realise . . . "——!" he would say, tearing up his copy, "now I'll have to write a column on Birmingham." When she was out of the room and his 'phone rang, he would try his best to ignore it, or he would get up and walk round it snarling like a dog preparing to worry it, or he would shout at me, "You answer it! It's you and your like that've made the lives of working men intolerable. If it hadn't been for your friend Alexander Bell . . ." Or he might pick it up, shout hastily, "He's no' in," and bang it down. Or if he was being amenable for once, he might say, "Mr. Mackay's butler speaking. Oh, it's you, Tovarich. Why didn't you say so? I nearly hung up on you."

How could anyone work out the K-coefficient of an atomic pile when a few feet away, in a voice so loud that he could have dispensed with the telephone, Mackay would be conducting a conversation with the "Duchess of Ditchwater" with all kinds of reflections on the manhood of the "Duke" and on the scions of the ducal house, although, all the time, "Her Grace" was some secretary at Transport House? Or when he would be speaking to some highly respectable spinster and inquiring solicitously for her offspring by name—usually

IAN AT WORK

—*by Vicky.*

slanderously christening them after public men? Or overhearing the labyrinthine excuses by which he would extricate himself from an engagement he did not want to keep or explaining why he had not kept one which he had forgotten all about?

He insisted on sitting next to the wall, partly to bank up the piles of papers and unanswered letters which overflowed his desk, but also to have the space on which to paste up his postcards ("All pictures fit to post"). And he had a vast assortment because everyone in Fleet Street, or so it seemed, sent him the most garish they could buy on holiday.

We all "lived" Mackay's Diary. There was a long period when, for me, the Diary began with coffee in the Kardomah before we ever reached the office. It was a kind of levee at which I would join him. By the time he got there he had read all his newspapers. He had walked from the Marylebone Road, via Wigmore Street, to collect his daily ration of two or three second-hand books and down Tottenham Court Road to collect a few "characters" and round various alleys and forgotten courts to collect atmosphere.

Over coffee, he would "get the news out of the way" with a vehement discourse on the morning's headlines, adorned with his personal views on the politicians, statesmen, diplomats or trade union leaders who had produced whatever crisis it was. Then he would do a mental cavort and swing the conversation round to his latest find—a phrase which he had found in a book for which he had probably bought it; the fourth leader in *The Times*, a favourite stamping-ground, or some obscure piece of news. And he would start fly-casting until I, or whoever might have joined us, would rise to the bait.

"Queer thing that scented ice which dropped out of the sky at Cardiff yesterday," he would say, "most mysterious!" And if I explained that it was certainly frozen hand-basin water from an aeroplane, he would rail reproachfully, "That's right. Kill a good story!" But I would not have done so.

Next morning his Diary would still start, "Not since manna
fell on the Children of Israel or since that day when Æschylus
was killed by a tortoise dropped by a passing eagle . . ."

Or someone would come over to the table and say, "Have
you heard, Ian, . . .?" and something which a frustrated
reporter had not managed to get in his own paper would be
grist to Mackay's mill.

Then he would sally forth. At this period, Ian had
acquired the girth and deportment of Mr. Chadband and,
with his scarf draped round his shoulders like a stole and his
coat flapping like a don's gown, he would sweep past the
tables exchanging ribaldries with his acquaintances. He
would pause to discuss the Persian situation with the policeman at the foot of Fetter Lane and the parlous state of
British cricket with the newspaper seller outside the post
office. His progress through the Temple would be interrupted
by his encounters with noted K.C.s. "And how is Serjeant
Buzfuz this morning?" "And what poor crittur is to be
hanged by your eloquent defence today?" or "Still appearing
in Jarndyce and Jarndyce?"

Preparations for the column were quite a ritual. He would
undress himself. He would take off his coat and jacket and
roll up his sleeves. (There was a time in the immediate
post-Wun Fang Yan period when he would also take out his
teeth.) He would take a bunch of pencils and stalk up and
down the room sharpening them, slicing off great swathes
and reviling the Buying Office because they did not provide
pencils to survive his onslaught. We were delivered from
these logging operations by a revolution: Mackay bought a
fountain pen and ordered a magnum of ink to go with it!

He would then enthrone himself, sweep a space clear on
his cluttered desk and grab a wad of copy-paper. He always
wrote his column, despising the artifices of a typewriter and
insisting that his handwriting was completely legible. Mostly

it was, but not always. Like the occasion when he had to devote the best part of another column to apologising to our colleague H. de Winton Wigley, whom his handwriting had described as "irresponsible" when it should have read "irrepressible."

There would be a temporary lull while he gazed transfixed into space, or rather into the *Star* offices opposite. Presently he would start to write and one false start after another would be crumpled up and thrown on the floor. Then, frustrated by his "intro.," he would find some excuse to resume his never-ending war with Ronald Walker.

This had been going on for years and anyone coming into the room would have thought that they were the bitterest of enemies instead of the best of friends and would not realise that these were just the hustings of "The Mackay Party" and "The Walker Party" each fighting on the most outrageous "programmes," caricaturing the politics of the day.

"Come the revolution," Mackay would roar, "and the tumbrils will roll for The Walker Party . . ."

Another lull and a few more crumpled sheets on the floor. Then with solemn dignity Ian would get up, robe himself and say to Maisie, "If anyone should deign to inquire for me, please inform them I have gone to Lambeth Palace to interview the Archbishop of Canterbury."

But there was a period when, thoroughly scared by his doctors, Ian renounced the taverns and took to bismuth to appease his duodenal. Everyone else had now, of course, become "wine-bibbers" and "toss-pots" and Ian would mix his stomach-mixture and say, "Will you join me in a beaker of belly-balm?"

The afternoon was when he "tried out" his ideas on us, or borrowed words. We had a scale of charges when he wanted us to provide a word—"Xenophobia," for instance, would be a ninepenny word. Or he would say, "Anyone swop me a fourpenny for 'sesquipedalian'?" And there were certain

words and phrases for which we threatened to fine him.
"Esoteric" was one; he loved it. And "space-time continuum,"
which I had carelessly left lying around one day.

He took the most outrageous liberties with his colleagues.
Walker was, for purposes of the Diary, "The Straffer of the
Stratosphere," Fothergill was "The Terror of the Tarmac"
and I was "The Atomic Sheik of Kalompong." We would
open our paper and find entirely apocryphal statements
attributed to us. There was one Diary which Gerald Barry,
as editor, took out after the first edition. It began with Ian
discovering Fothergill reading the *Magnet* (quite untrue) and
then, with greater or less degree of verity, recounted what all
his colleagues were supposed to be reading, finishing up with
Geoffrey Cox reading Karl Marx's *Das Kapital* because Karl
was so sound on sheep-farming! If the editor was concerned
about our feelings he need not have worried. Most people
guyed by Mackay were rather like the man who boasted that
he had been kicked by George III.

The intervention by Barry was an occasion for another
of that long series of "From Mackay to the Editor" letters.
These, in the original versions, were diatribes, equalled only
by the Biblical curse in Deuteronomy. Even the final versions,
as modified by Maisie taking out the expletives, and the rest
of us removing the actionable slanders, were masterpieces of
invective, the effect of which was later ruined by Ian meeting
the victim and saying, with a grin, "Like my last effort?"

Anyway, these periodic eruptions, usually following some
misadventure of his copy, were memorable occasions: for
one thing, Ian dictated the letters—a thing he never did
otherwise—and would stamp up and down the room bellow-
ing his dictation. " 'Dear Sir'—that'll shake him for a start!
'Never in a long experience of morons and microbe-minds,
nitwits, half-wits, quarter-wits and sub-editors . . .' " And if
any one of us tried to temper the worst of his abuse by saying,

"I wouldn't say that, Ian," he would turn on him and roar, "Of course, ye wouldna', you craven, lily-livered wage-slave." But the tornadoes always passed without any serious damage to anyone concerned.

Everything was copy to Ian. He would wander over to my desk and pick up some publication and the next day one would find "Next to the *Racing Pigeon* or the *World's Fair*, the most exciting journals that I read each week are the *Lancet, Nature* and the *British Medical Journal*." Or he would ask us about our friends and their foibles. For instance, he once asked me if any of my friends had a favourite pipe, and I told him that Lord Boyd Orr smoked one which had a stem which did not even pretend to belong to its bowl. This, to Ian, became a pipe which Boyd Orr had got on his wedding-day and which he had smoked ever since on the principle of George Washington's axe which had had six different heads and ten different hafts.

It was always disconcerting to introduce Ian to a friend or a distinguished visitor. He would invariably bow and shake hands with old-world courtesy and say, "I am honoured to meet you, sir, but distressed to find you in such disreputable company."

Even when he was away on his travels, none of us was safe because we could never be sure what he was going to say on his open postcards which he wrote with as much verve and gusto and disrespect as he wrote his Diary. One of his last described how he had contrived to get himself mistaken for a certain duke at Northolt Airport and how the people of the French village where he was staying were under the impression that he was an English bishop and he was scandalised that they were not scandalised.

The Room never was, and never could be, the same again after his death. We all aged considerably, because that boyish exuberance with which he infected us all went with him.

The Man from Wick

BY

IVOR BROWN

*Ivor Brown, associate editor and dramatic critic of "The Observer,"
has written many authoritative books on Shakespeare, dramatic criticism,
and the English language.*

I FIRST met Ian Mackay on the fringe of Putney Heath. It was at a party given by that great enjoyer of life, as well as student of politics, Herbert Sidebotham. He had met Ian in the Gallery of the House of Commons and, since he had an eye for all the good, rich things of this world, he naturally made a friend of him.

It was there explained to me that this huge, shock-headed fellow had come out of my own country and, indeed, from the same north-eastern corner of it. But his north was farthest north. He was one of the caterans of Caithness, the man from Wick. If he did not agree with Sir Archibald Sinclair in the reasonable mildness of Liberal politics, he had at least, in boyhood, poached the Sinclair salmon.

One of G.B.S.'s working-class characters, when advised not to breed so furiously, retorted that abstinence in this matter was against his religion. So Ian Mackay would have replied to a suggestion that he abandon the lifting of fish by the claim that such a course would be against his principles. He was a Socialist and held that salmon should be, in Wordsworth's phrase, "a joy in widest commonalty spread."

Moreover he looked like a man of the woods and watercourses and not at all like those prim, precise Gallery correspondents of the nineteen-twenties who had so long been peering down through their pince-nez at the drab arena of a dull debate that they had a permanently downcast look. Ian seemed to have arrived at St. Stephen's out of prehistory, blown in on the snowy blasts of Boreas, the snell north-easter, and yet quite able to keep himself warm by his own high spirits.

To call him a Pict or a Celt would involve me in one of those ethnological mysteries with which Scottish history begins and which have produced a whole library of tedious speculation and argle-bargle. So let us call him a character who blew into a Fleet Street where G. K. Chesterton was still to be seen with a large glass of red wine in the Rainbow Tavern after he had (somewhat sketchily) edited the week's *New Witness*.

Remembering the famous Chestertonian song of the rolling English drunkard who made the rolling English road and got to Birmingham by way of Beachy Head, one might say of Ian, in all accuracy and sobriety, that he got from Wick to Westminster by way of Plymouth Hoe. In covering, by his education in Wick and his early journalism for the *Western Morning News*, the length of Britain from Dunnet Head to South Devon, he acquired some of that glorious store of supposedly useless information which he turned to profitable use in the omniscient gossip of his later journalism and in his appearances before the microphone.

Wick is neither a cushion on which to recline nor a beauty spot on which to gaze. Its historic exports have been men, fish and paving-stones. The streets of London are in its debt for some of their hardiness. The young Ian was an abounding and excessive creature from the start. He claimed to have been the ace of top-whippers, with a great top called Habakkuk, "fat as an alderman and shining like a rainbow," which was the champion spinner of the town. His kite, Clipper of the Clouds, was also, in his opinion, a monarch. But at trundling the hoop he was defeated by his own adored one, Dulcie Alexander, fleeter of foot, he thought, than Swinburne's "fleet-foot kid."

It is a nice stroke of fortune which mixes the strange with the stranger. For a boy with a light in his eyes and a long nose for the curious to be employed in the chemist's shop of William Gow Miller was really good fortune. Miller was a dandy—among the herrings and the paving-stones. He looked "like one of the Cheeryble Brothers dressed in Beau Brummell's fanciest suit." He travelled extensively in Europe during his summer holidays. He then returned to drink Chianti in Caithness, to smoke perfumed cigars among the kippers, and to take jabs of cocaine in the manner of the earlier Holmes. Under such guidance did Ian learn to mix a pill and prepare a purge for the costive citizens of Caledonia's tip. The English think of the Scots as very serious folk. As a matter of fact the country has had a commendable output of eccentrics and Gow was not unique.

Wick then had no electric light and was short of plumbing. It was bleak and, though the light and plumbing came, it remained bleak. When Ian revisited it in 1938 he did so with no lift of the spirit. The town had gone dry under local option and the drinkers had to travel to Lybster or Thurso for their revels. The harbour life was nearly dead. It was all empty and strange to the man in search of his youth. "I met few of my boyhood friends," he wrote, "as most of my generation were either killed in the war or have wandered away to the ends of the earth. Probably I would meet more of them in Manitoba or Queensland. On the whole my visit was a sad business and I don't think I shall ever go back again."

I don't know whether he did. But he went back to Scotland frequently in the year or two before his death to take part in "Town Forum" broadcasts, in which he was extremely popular and successful. The fact that he had no affection for Scottish Nationalism did not lose him friends even among the faithful Home Rulers. His tongue was always quick with an answer, while his mind was always stocked with an astonishing amount of miscellaneous facts. Perhaps with a few fictions too. But, considering the huge catalogue of oddities and coincidences and queer topographical associations on which he drew for his talk or writing, he was, as far as I know, extremely accurate. His truth was stranger than fiction and it was actually true.

So into a society that becomes ever more assimilated came this unpredictable man. Fleet Street seems to me a much duller place than when I first knew it: the high cost of drinking has put regular tavern gatherings outside the reach of the young. Such assemblies as those of the *London Mercury* men in Poppins Court or the Friday night dinners of the Scots Club are unthinkable now. Accordingly, if there are rare characters about, one doesn't hear of them or meet them. Drink is not necessary to companionship, however much it may help, but assemblance is. And modern journalism does not assemble as it did. Ian Mackay belonged to the natural assemblers, and with his going went a great mountain of character and friendliness.

London has always needed and welcomed the stranger. The journalist from Wick bestrode the Cockney scene and enriched it. It is odd that a man from the coldest corner of Caledonia should have been so worthy to have walked out of a Dickens novel. And what more cordial compliment can be paid to anyone than to say that he was good enough to have been created by that hand of English bounty?

Ian's London Lore

BY

JAMES BONE

*James Bone, London editor of the "Manchester Guardian" from 1911
to 1945, is an authority on London lore and has published many
delightful books on the subject.*

A WALLOP of Dr. Johnson in his passion for certainty
and argument, a flash of Falstaff's bawdry and misadventure, a queer personal humility towards those
whose gifts (often less than his own) he admired, a torrent
of Robert Burns' "A Man's a Man for a' That" flood-brown
democracy, an insatiable appetite and vast crop for facts
and out-of-the-way facts that others didn't know, suggesting
Mr. Whitaker (of the Almanack) himself: these were to
me most of the components of Ian Mackay the journalist—if
you add to that a bit of yourself that you were always,
sometimes uncomfortably, realising; for Mackay was
humanity afoot, afoot and footloose.

No one really knows London. Even Dickens didn't. The
qualities that let one know what Max Beerbohm called the
Parish of St. James do not help much with Poplar or Walham
Green even if one had lodged there, and in socially lived
areas like Bermondsey and Kentish Town the problems and
embarrassments are not, like their cinema fare, the same.

Mackay's London was far more extensive than that of
most students of London for he knew much of it closely on
the political Labour side and it gave him a vast basis. He had
tramped many districts gathering the harvest of his unquiet
eye in times of disaster or strikes. An entertainer himself, he
knew London entertainment widely from the free-and-easy

in pub back parlours where it survived here and there to the
T. S. Eliot and Ustinov conclaves and was a genuine authority on the music hall. "Locals" had few secrets to Ian, and
he could name, and describe, a surprising number and even
ascribe an explanation of the strangest pub name.

I suppose there was, as he contended, a tavern in Wands-
worth called "The Friendly Zulu"; his explanation sounded
plausible enough. I remember how quickly he fastened on to
and enlarged a little about Dickens one day at the Dickensian
Grapes Tavern at Limehouse Causeway through a letter the
innkeeper had recently received from Vancouver.

It was on the occasion of a trip down the river to welcome
Chris Morley, the American author and columnist, where
Ian and he opened a grand friendship. Ian was the first man
on the Thames Police launch to discover that two great
seamen there were the only men aboard who had never seen
the London river before, indeed had never come beyond
Tilbury! One of them was an admiral who had commanded
H.M.S. *Renown* and the other had been an extra master in
sail and commodore of the Anchor Line!

Retirement from Fleet Street in 1945 deprived me from
seeing much of Ian Mackay when he was becoming London's
greatest and liveliest columnist on events of the day, and it
was only then that the breadth, particularly, and ever-
surprising richness of his London knowledge flooded upon us.
As an amateur on the subject myself I was always coming on
something in his writings that made me think "now where
on earth did he get that from," some reference perhaps to a
particular lamp-post in Portland Place where Gladstone and
Carlyle had shaken hands for the last time, or something
like that. But when I tackled Ian he could always quote his
reference. His expertness on the Sherlock Holmes saga was
particularly impressive—it even went the length of setting
Conan Doyle right.

But the point I would like to make is that this knowledge comprised both mortals and immortals and that it seldom failed. At Rembrandt's tercentenary the University of Leyden conferred on writers who had written well on that matter the degree of "Doctors of Rembrandt": Ian Mackay, though not as deeply informed as Dr. Gomme or Dr. Steen Rasmussen, well deserved to be a "Doctor of London." Sad it is that he had never concentrated his knowledge and fancy into a book on London!

But if I may turn aside for the moment from Ian's own London lore to the London lore he created for the Londoners themselves I would like to give one example. For instance, can the Café Royal, rich as it is in legend, have many more curious encounters than this?

Mackay told me that one night there after sitting at a table, not playing dominoes, but drinking and talking with a friend, he rose to go and a heavy man who had been sitting nearby came to him and said, "You'll be Ian Mackay?" Mackay admitted it. "Well," asked the stranger, "what kind of Mackay are ye—are ye a black Mackay or a red Mackay?" "I told him," said Ian, "that I didn't know and I didn't care what colour of a Mackay I was. There were more important things! He then asked me if I knew what the crest of the Mackays was. I said that I didn't and didn't care what it was. He said that it was a hand holding an open dagger, and what was the motto of the Mackays? I told him 'no,' and he said that it was 'strike home'! 'Now did I know,' he asked, 'that being so, the one thing a Mackay wanted?' I said, 'Not a glimmer.' 'The back of a friend,' he said, 'that's all to ye!' 'I asked him what he was,' said Ian, 'but he was off.' "

Whoever he was he had certainly spoken to a Mackay who did only kindnesses behind the back of a friend.

Mackay had done much exploration and research into the

village of Fleet Street and its congeries. At a Press gathering memorable to at least one of those present Ian said:

"I am one of the few people here who can really claim to be a genuine villager of that astonishing and completely unknown village that lies tucked away in the side streets between the King Lud and the Devereux."

His speech then took a personal turn, for the occasion happened to be my own farewell to Fleet Street, but, as it was in a way his farewell, too, to living in Fleet Street, it may be recalled here. He continued:

"For over twenty years now, James and I have not only worked together but lived together in the Street. And his home and mine were both blown up by the Luftwaffe on the same night. . . . I myself am being turned out tomorrow and it looks as if I shall have to sink to the level of Regent's Park."

And now to us, the aged and retired, who live in country villages, shuffling along Fleet Street in our revivifications we shall still glimpse that tall rocky figure with its bristling bushel of hair that never hid the light beneath it, the visage like Cape Wrath and eyes, changeful and at times tender as a summer in Skye, and somehow I shall associate his memory with another devoted unforgettable figure of Fleet Street who, too, had to the end something of eternal youth—Robert Lynd.

Ian at Sea

BY

GILES

*B*EING *late for first-day-at-sea lifeboat drill, I was taking the palatial "Queen Mary" staircase two at a time when I collided with an obstruction which turned out to be Ian Mackay.*

He was travelling towards the lifeboat station at a very slow, shuffling pace, caused partly by the trailing tangled tapes of his lifebelt which he was wearing back to front, and partly by a pair of very unwilling slippered feet.

Although I had not seen Ian for several years, there was only time for a "How you doing, Ian?" and a reply, "Fine, Giles, me boy— made the grade—GOUT, first class, both feet."

I had the drill and a lecture on what we were to do if the "Mary" took a dive, was told the number of my lifeboat in case of such an emergency, and was dismissed half an hour later knowing full well that if the "Mary" did anything so ungracious I should make a bee-line for the nearest lifeboat like everybody else.

Returning to the gin palaces of the upper decks I met Ian still coming downstairs on his way to drill.

He had not made the bottom of the first flight!

THE DRILL-GRIM'S PROGRESS

165

Ian the Ocean Traveller

BY

DON IDDON

*Don Iddon, American columnist of the "Daily Mail," and a prolific
writer on man and affairs.*

IAN did not expect to die so young.

We crossed the Atlantic together in the *Queen Mary* in
1948 and we both did a lot of talking and listening. I
remember sitting on the promenade deck with Ian, who was
nursing gout in his foot, and he said, "Gout is supposed to
be a rich man's affliction but I'm not rich and never will be.
The *News Chronicle* has been good to me and I can do more or
less what I want. There's this American trip, for instance.
The *News Chronicle* doesn't pay fancy salaries like the *Mail*
and the *Express*, but there's stability and security."

He winced as the pain in his foot shot up his leg and then
said, "I'm not getting any younger but I think I've got
fifteen years more journalism left in me."

Ian looked well on that voyage. He was a good sailor and
hobbled about audaciously even in rough weather when the
decks were slanting and the bars swaying. We had a good
passenger list—Sir Ralph Richardson and Claude Rains
the actors, Giles the cartoonist, James and Frank Butler the
sports writers, and Jack Solomons the fish merchant and
prize-fight promoter. Ian dominated our group.

I have never known a more erudite man. Even Ralph
Richardson who has played so much Shakespeare bowed to
Mackay as a scholar. Ian had a tremendous admiration for
Richardson. I used to play table tennis with the actor and
occasionally beat him while Ian refereed. Ian would say,

after Richardson had gone, "There goes Britain's greatest actor and that means the world's."

Ian was quite a booster for Britain on this transatlantic voyage and during his American journey. He was passionately Scottish, of course, but decided to join forces with the English, the Welsh and the Northern Irish for the purposes of debate or argument with the Americans. As a Left Winger (he used to call himself an old-fashioned Liberal—to which the rather obvious reply was that he was liberal with old-fashioneds) Ian had not extravagant affection for the booming American capitalist economy. We would talk in the smoking room and I would say, "We can't keep taking aid from the United States. It's been going on and on and there seems no end to it. It's humiliating. Beaverbrook was right—we should never have taken a dime or a dollar in the first place."

Ian said, "I expect to live to see the time when Britain will be sending Bundles for America and bailing the Americans out." He never did.

Mackay, the journalist and political philosopher, thought the British Socialists were on the right track and American big business was likely to go off the rails. I don't think he would have liked working in America for long as a correspondent. He didn't like the glittering glossy bars aboard the *Queen Mary*, or the cocktail lounges in Manhattan. He liked old pubs and old ale.

There have been many stories about Ian's capacity for drink. On our voyage he drank only Bass, although the whisky and champagne were flowing around the Solomons, Butler, Giles and Iddon party. Ian seemed to be able to make a pint of Bass last half an hour and lubricate at least three anecdotes.

This was his first and only journey to the United States, and in New York he spent a good deal of time in the Little

Cottage, a bar resembling an English pub, near the Associated Press building. The beer is served in mugs. It is not a chic or fancy place. Despite his gout Ian disdained bar stools, planted his swollen foot on the brass rail and declaimed on British journalism.

He was nonplussed and overwhelmed by the size of the American newspapers. The first Sunday he was here he telephoned from his hotel room for the *New York Times* and the *New York Herald Tribune* and when the bellboy brought them up he shouted from his bed, "Push them under the door." The Sunday editions of American newspapers are multi-paged and mammoth and only strong men can carry them. They would have had to take the door out.

Ian thought the newspaper writing here was verbose and involved. He did not like the heavy thinkers and he did not like the gossip gadflies. At the time of Ian's visit Walter Winchell, the millionaire commentator and columnist, was saying some violent things about Britain. I remember that Ernest Bevin was ill and Winchell's comment was, "Nothing trivial, I hope." This infuriated Ian so much I thought he was going to hobble over to the Stork Club and beat up Winchell.

Throughout Ian's American stay the anti-British campaign raged. The *New York Post* was calling Britain "A malignant cancer among nations" and editorially describing Ernie Bevin as "a bloody man, a Nazi." Winchell was calling us "The Brutish, the ratzis" and worse.

This sort of abuse puzzled and wounded Ian Mackay, who was a gentle man despite the occasional flares of temper, the shock of hair, the eyes that could be fierce. But he trekked across the country from New York to San Francisco riding the streamliners, talking and listening to the people, and when he finally left—of course, it could have been coincidence—the hate-Britain campaign over the Palestine issue seemed to have subsided.

I find it hard to recall whether it was aboard the *Queen Mary* or in New York that Ian told his various tales to me. He was, though a great talker, a modest man. His name had been plastered in huge letters across the sides of the London buses and I said, rather enviously, "How do you feel about it? You must get quite a kick every time you look at a bus."

Ian said, "Why, the damn fools. The day the posters came out on the buses they didn't print my piece. Lost it, or didn't like it or something."

Perhaps of all the contributors to this book I knew Ian least. When I first went to Fleet Street I was twenty-one and Ian was a great figure then. He used to swing into Poppins with Frank Owen and Arthur Christiansen the fabulous *Daily Express* editor, and I used to look at the three great men and maybe dream a bit. It was not until our transatlantic crossing that Ian and I came to know each other better and became friends.

Some of our fellow-passengers used to call Ian the scholar and me the show man. This is a little tribute from the show man to the scholar.

Ian in America

BY

STANLEY BURCH

Stanley Burch is the New York correspondent of the "News Chronicle."

THE gaiety started in a telephone booth a minute from Ian's landing in America and it spread from him and struck laughter in return from the Atlantic coast to California's Golden Gate and back again.

Of all the unpromising places in which he had only to peer to find enchantment there was none more unlikely than the Manhattan Telephone Directory. But when he opened it on the New York waterfront to find his office's number, the first of all the New World's laughs swept him. LONDON NEWS CHRONICLE (*a pub*), it said.

Mightily encouraged, Mackay drove across the seedy West Side, past the Broadway shop windows with their hand-painted nude-splattered neckwear, to Rockefeller Center.

"I promised Robin* to be good," he announced. And good he was (he stuck to beer manfully in a land of hard liquor)—though across all the States in which he shook his noble hair they had never known goodness expressed in so much fun and gusto and un-American activity.

His doctor had given him some last-minute cautionary tales on how he should behave (he said). But within a few days he came roaring in through the door with a letter from home. "My doctor's dead," he cried in triumph. "After all that—*I've outlived him!*"

He outlived most of us, in the other sense, as he tramped

* Robin Cruikshank, editor of the *News Chronicle*.

170

and rode a New York bursting with revelation for his mind, and fodder for his Diary. His staunch and stumpy little pencil came out with the regularity of a subway train to feed those battered little notebooks.

"That's good, I'll use that!" he said delightedly as he recorded a bright little remark by a New York waitress who under his kindly interrogation told him she came from Denmark. Weeks later it came out in his Diary, "As a Chinese waiter told me in San Francisco . . ." There was many a transposition like that as his tale went off in airmailed batches to Bouverie Street; and how richly Nature was always improved on.

Yes, he would like to see a wayside tavern in nearby Westchester County which carried a sign proclaiming it as "the Home of the First Cocktail." He wrote it down, of course, with the date. What knocked me back when I read it in the paper was his reminder of the "odd fact"—one I had never noticed in all the years—that it was the date of the Declaration of Independence. Some day I shall go back to check that.

Pub crawls around New York prepared him and fortified him valuably for the thousands of miles of travel lying ahead of him. He looked around one of the cocktail lounges of suburban Bronxville—at a score of rich men and the sons and daughters of rich men. "If this were any pub in England," he said, "the people would all be different. You know there'd be some *characters*. They all look alike here." They did; and they gazed in fascination on the character in their midst, with his bold and searching eyes and his fabulous head.

From Long Island villages to the valley towns of the Hudson and the noisy dens on 51st Street, the locals edged nearer to catch some of the flow of talk streaming from the man. They had heard of Dr. Johnson, perhaps of Chesterton.

But to see and hear it in action, in America, in the mid-twentieth century . . .

How the cocktail parties sparkled on the penthouse terraces of Greenwich Village, in the sunset; in the apartments of literary folk uptown. Ian made the rich red wine of Socialism shame the Martinis; he transformed the pallid inanities of party chatter into something exciting; he even struck answering fire from minds long unkindled; and he astonished admiring women by a direct and penetrating gaze they had clearly not experienced before in such a babble.

Many of these Americans tried to analyse the impact of their extraordinary visitor. They got tied up in foggy abstract phrases that didn't get within miles of the truth. What they missed mostly was a quite simple truth. The truth, I mean, that the sort of Americans who frequent that kind of party run to types—types of personality, types of behaviour, types of outlook, types of wit; while he was a whole man.

The tolerance behind the uncompromising assertion, the gentleness behind the unconventionality, the integrity that bound the infinite variety, the singleness that underlay the fantastic ranging imagination . . . this was a new and an exciting phenomenon to many a New Yorker long slave to sophisticated, selfconscious little stereotypes.

And while it was almost impossible for Ian to "shock," he was so extraordinarily good at shaking people. Like the couple who had on their table a conspicuously laid copy of newly published *The Heart of the Matter*. They were clever young people, who had obviously planned a clever discussion of the book, with many a smart psychological ray to illuminate it. All this was stillborn in a moment of terrible silence at Ian's first comment. "I can never be interested," said he, "in any book that assumes there's anything special or peculiar about a man going to bed with a woman."

To any who came to him with the inevitable desire for his

first impression of their exciting city, Ian would say, "The first sight of New York can be no surprise to anyone who's ever seen *King Kong*"; then he would roll out some tenth or hundredth impression that nobly enriched his listener. His grandmother got her mentions, never doubt. And British politics acquired a fine new significance in the minds of those who reached the elbow of this remarkable interpreter.

When, in full flow, Ian suspected some scepticism in the eyes of his listeners—some hint that fancy was glorifying fact —he would subdue it magnificently by a single shining proof that the most outrageous things are the most likely to be true. He had been told (he explained) that he was a liar in telling so many personal anecdotes about Puccini—he "couldn't possibly" have been there at all those places, London, Leeds, Glasgow, Manchester, Bristol. "What that unbelieving fellow didn't know was that I was touring with Puccini. I was his publicity man." Confidence came back to American hearts; they couldn't catch this man out.

It was pelting rain with horrible, tropical intensity the night he was due to leave for the Western trek—and it nearly wrecked his whole scheme. There were no taxis on Broadway, where he had been shopping for presents. We were sodden, dripping creatures when we reached his hotel room. "I'm not going," Ian announced. "I'd get my gout. I'll cable Robin and explain, and then push off later."

Reservations were then extraordinarily hard to get on transcontinental trains, and elaborate hotel arrangements had been made in California. A cancellation would have meant an awful mess. Time pressed.

It took us long blandishment (my wife and I) to persuade him to give himself a restoring rub-down in the bathroom, while we got out some dry clothes and finished his packing. We got him down the Grand Central tunnel to his train and his berth just before it pulled out for the Pacific, and told the gentle Pullman attendant of his charge's importance, and his need for the best of service.

Sure enough, the story when it came out had raised magic from that sorry start. While we had been plodding damply home he had established a glorious discovery linking Wick, via Africa, with that thundering train. "The Black Mackay," the Diary proclaimed; and the Negro's name, he swore ever after, had really been Mackay.

In Reno he found a waterfall of whisky; in San Francisco and Hollywood a thousand delights. Most of them he communicated to his readers, the best he had to preserve for private conversation. The strip-tease joints, for instance, around the Chicago stockyards, later to be made world-renowned by the Eisenhower and Adlai Stevenson conventions.

As the all-night shifts of faded women did their weary stripping standing on the bar (he would recount) the customers had to watch for the moment to skid empty glasses between their legs for refilling. He looked up at one performer when she had made her final discard, to see inscribed on her flanks "Read the *Chicago Tribune*."

He brought back one angry memory of California to darken his ecstasies. The girl at the hotel who told a guest over the phone one morning that they did not serve breakfast for two in a bedroom booked by one. "That place should be blacklisted," was his snorted advice to Easterners.

A laughing ambassador was Ian Mackay. There are uncounted Americans today who, because they met him, think not of sterling convertibility and nationalisation problems when Britain is mentioned—but of humanity and fertile fun, of dauntless spirit and uncontaminated loyalties, and of cleansing unconquerable gaiety.

He came to America too late. He left too soon. And he never wrote a book about it, the old rascal.

Ian as Broadcaster

BY

SIR COMPTON MACKENZIE

Sir Compton Mackenzie is one of Britain's most versatile authors, poets, broadcasters and script-writers. Former literary critic of the "Daily Mail."

I T was not my fortune to meet Ian Mackay until a comparatively short time before he was so suddenly taken from us. Therefore I can pay only the briefest tribute to that large, warm and lovable personality. It has been for me too literally *Ave atque vale*. I was lucky enough to serve with him once in the team for the Scottish equivalent of "Any Questions" which is called "A Matter of Opinion." It was a great experience, for he was the perfect mate for such an occasion, the success of which depends on the ability of the team to combine well.

Nowadays I have a list of people the presence of any of whom at these unscripted broadcast discussions keeps me from accepting the invitation to take part, because I know that the audience will be aware of something wrong and will be themselves uncomfortable.

The first essential is never to "hog" the microphone when others have something to say. In my experience nearly everybody goes on too long. Conversation should be the aim, not speech-making. Ian Mackay never held on to the microphone for a moment when he divined, as he always did immediately, that somebody else had something to say.

He had every reason to know that a Scottish audience was prepared to listen to him as long as he liked to go on, but he never presumed on this, and he never cashed in by saying exactly what his audience expected him to say in a stylised manner of delivery. In a word he was not willing to sacrifice his matter in order to preserve his manner.

We are apt to think of the men of Caithness as tough and dour. Ian Mackay could be tough, but I never heard or saw him dour. Fleet Street loved him and he loved Fleet Street.

It was my privilege to have him as chairman when the Press Club entertained some of us to dinner, and of course the evening was a success. If the Press Club had been entertaining two or three tailors' dummies to dinner with Ian Mackay in the chair, the evening would have been a success.

Others will write of him more intimately than I can hope to do. David Keir and I had planned to make him a member of the Savile where I was hoping to see much of a man who had come late into my life and yet who from the moment I met him seemed to have been in it for years. Alas, the swift blow fell and instead of writing to tell the Election Committee what an ideal member he would be I am writing these few lines to declare what a wonderful chap he was.

PART THREE

Ian Rusticated

BY

JOHN PUDNEY

John Pudney, poet, fiction writer, dramatist and journalist, former correspondent of the "News Chronicle" and book critic "Daily Express."

As one who owed not a little adult education to the zestful, garrulous, over-informative spirit of Ian Mackay, I always in my youth regarded him as the epitome of urbanism. When I, in my twenties, first sat at his feet, he would declare that life began at Temple Bar and that the world to the west of that invisible landmark was of no concern at all. When he held forth on the meaning of words, or spouted poetry, or declaimed about the "shining orb of the docker's tanner," or dilated on the Fleet Street taverns, he always seemed to me to speak as the most confirmed metropolitan.

His very appearance bore this out. He was the wild man in town clothes. A fantastic tie or a shaggy pullover might relieve the untidy, almost clerical garments that hung about him. The overloaded pockets stuffed with papers, cuttings and correspondence in wads ready to be dragged out and quoted from added to the general shapelessness and underlined the townee atmosphere. Later life brought a measure of style and elegance to Ian's outward appearance which in those days was splendidly lacking.

My early impression was that Ian was always in black—black albeit a little rusty from timeless sojourn in the city. The thought of Ian in country garments was inconceivable. The sight of Ian reluctantly travelling with us as far west as the Café Royal was rare enough. It was, in fact, almost as a joke that I first invited him to visit us in the first country cottage we ever possessed. His ready acceptance of that invitation to remote Essex filled us with something approaching panic—that kind of social panic that comes over one who is about to entertain a tweed-clad aunt in London, a vegetarian at a dinner party, a Siamese prince in a suburb.

Ian perhaps would deplore mud. He would bump his head upon those detestable *olde worlde* beams we had. He would feel at a loss in the homespun company in the single bar at the local. He might indeed be one of those awkward country guests who refuse to go outdoors and who, wearing dark glasses, stare dolefully out of the windows watching the inevitable chores of chicken-feeding or bringing in the vegetables.

Ian arrived, of course, in his blackish clothes. He brought a pile of reading matter and our hearts sank lest he should be one of those guests who come thus armed in the townee belief that newspapers and periodicals never circulate in country places.

It rained. How it rained! How persistently, for that matter, did he bump his head! Yet what an interest and an understanding he showed for that little old inconveniently snug place. What a lasting impression he effortlessly made on that homespun company in the local. What mud we went through and how unconcernedly.

He flattered us a good deal by recalling this visit in somewhat more detail than it deserved. When we moved to an Essex farmhouse where no heads were bumped, Ian came again, compared the new home with the old appreciatively and with much perception and took the local by storm. I found then that the blackish clothes were no hindrance to a spirit that genuinely revered country things, and that the metropolitan manner was no stumbling block to rustic relationships. Ian not only went down well in the pub. He might have been born and bred in the place.

Ian in the country was, in fact, a social acquisition. He could talk nightingales. He could talk cows. He was at his ease over prices as well as rates of pay. I toured Vernon Bartlett's constituency with him in the hot days of the 'thirties. He came with me to Kent in the days when our world was cooling off in the 'forties, and I was fighting a rural constituency myself. Nobody ever looked less likely to understand rural problems: nobody ever in my experience assimilated them with a more ready understanding.

Since the war, when we lived in Kent, Ian came to see us several times. Many people he met in the village would ask when he was coming again. Not because they had read his column or heard him on the radio, but because the man in town clothes—less rusty and more elegant than in former times—had managed to stick in their thoughts.

But it was not by holding forth on the world east of Temple Bar, but by that ready curiosity about people and their affairs and that charming articulateness about anything under the sun that made him one of the most versatile journalists of our time.

In later years, in fact, one came to realise that Ian loved the country in the best possible way. Not just as a weekend spectacle but with a deep understanding that included much more than superficial æsthetic appreciation.

Yet I must confess that, though he might concede an appearance in shirt-sleeves on a very hot day, I never saw him looking anything but uncompromisingly urban.

PRESS CLUB ÉTUDE

—by Cummings.

Willow and Wine

BY

JOHN ARLOTT

John Arlott, the detective who became one of Britain's most distinctive broadcasters, poet, author, cricket commentator and writer; now on the London "Evening News."

WHEN I first met Ian Mackay—only five or six years ago—I had an affection for him which is only possible in one brought up in a home which took his paper every morning. He had been, for me, a name, two words in heavy type at the top of a column. He became a man I met and relished, then one to be envied for his gifts, and for the fact that he had received that coveted accolade of journalism—"a column of his own."

Finally, that night when I looked casually at that corner of "The Feathers" and knew that, this time, he was not in some other town, county, country or continent, but gone, I looked with the incomprehension of a friend.

He had about him, for me—and not for me alone—the stuff of relishable legend. That shock of hair might not be barbered into discipline, nor his jaw permanently dentured into the look of other men. He could not waste good living time on knotting a tie "properly," nor on the adjustment of collar-points to a common plane.

"Did you know Ranji had a glass eye?" he once asked me in the middle of a discussion on Bowdler. I did not know. Ian did. He had recently had an operation on an eye and, by that mysterious divination of uncataloguable information which was one of his major journalistic gifts, he knew about men with one eye—and, because he was not a card-indexer, he had spread his knowledge to cricketers with deformities. I remembered a glass-eyed Test cricketer and preened myself. Ian had found one with a blind eye.

He had needed—professionally too—to be tough: he could put on an air of toughness. He could never *be* truly tough because he was too sensitive. He could never ask you the tritely courteous question because he could not waste questions. He was a good talker because he was a good listener. He was a Scot who valued words too highly to treat them as dross.

We sat one night after dinner, Ian, Teddy Knox, Clarice Mayne, Ronnie Waldman, Gerard Fay, my wife and myself. The talk moved soon to the variety stage. Ian fitted in gaps of dates, names and titles, years and bills, not recalled as a feat of memory, but as part of the background of enjoyment. This was one of the pools of his ocean. He was an eager listener when Teddy or Clarice remembered; a gentle critic because, where there was quality to appreciate, he was constitutionally incapable of overlooking it.

Not long before he and Rosemary Say were married he asked her, "Would you like a honeymoon trip across France, through Italy, Yugoslavia, Greece and on round the edge of the Mediterranean to Egypt?" Clearly, there was only one answer for a girl who was going to marry Ian Mackay. "Or," he went on, "would you like furniture—sideboards and wardrobes and that sort of thing—like other women have?" For a girl who was going to marry Ian Mackay there was no change of mind.

He created a mythology so imaginatively true that no technical expert could have discredited it—out of the cricket that he had watched. Although he was, so far as we know, not a practising cricketer beyond waste-land standard, we relished it far more deeply than the wisdom of many self-declared *afficionados* of the game. Ian perceived, always, not only the man under the flannels but also that man in relation to his cricket. He understood that theirs is a world which becomes dull if it is real; that it is, in essence, a fairy-tale kingdom—and he knew how rare and valuable the true fairy tale is. Indeed, he himself often told fairy tales, true fairy tales, because they were concerned with the finest truth, which is the truth of imagination.

He liked nothing better, of a summer afternoon, than watching cricket at Lord's. At one time he had a flat overlooking Lord's and, when he heard the quiet noise of cricket over the wall, it was hard for him to pass on to Fleet Street. Yet he was no "Lord's snob." The presence there of a great cricketer—which is, as he observed, one great in character as in technique—would as regularly draw him to the Oval. It was at the Oval that he watched the magnificent cricket of Jack Hobbs in the 'twenties, and developed his own feeling for the game.

He was an enthusiast for enthusiasms. There were so many worlds. Many of them were, of necessity, unknown to him for years until someone opened a door on a fresh one, and gave Ian a fierce need to understand it, to ask about it, to learn to appreciate its new values. Yet, there was an implacable Mackay, hard and unyielding as a flint when anyone attacked or—even by inference—slighted the ethical and humane standards he held. There the Calvinist stood up and fought.

He was a journalist and a Scot, therefore he relished Scotch, and frequently refreshed himself with beer. Perhaps the greatest factual tribute that can be paid to him is that Ian in his cups was the same Ian as you met in the morning—essentially the same, if perhaps even more appreciative, inclined to see things even *more*, more than life-size.

He came to the tasting, understanding and appreciation of wine with the delight of a child. That was the delight he preserved, the delight of a child, its mental palate always clear to appreciate the new. His respect for words would not allow him to adopt the hackneyed jargon of literary winesmanship. He sought for the word which defined a wine, not that which merely approved or condemned.

Put a glass of wine in his hand and he would look, smell and taste with the interest of one who is exploring. He was not to be hoodwinked by years or labels or names. If he liked a wine he could tell you why and, if the experts did not agree, perhaps he had not yet reached their standard of discrimination. He was willing to study—and delightful he found the study—to reach their level: meanwhile, but quite undogmatically, he liked the wine he liked.

People would always tell him the expert details of their own world because they were convinced of his interest in it: he could absorb that information because, too wise to pretend to knowledge, he allowed his natural sympathy to show through. He had, that is to say, an infallible feeling for other men's "shop," which he recognised for the true metal that it is.

He was, perhaps, the last of the great line of English essayists. He was handicapped by the fact that the postwar newspaper has space for news but not for manœuvre. Ian Mackay saw round corners, and he liked to be fair to a topic, liked to appraise it, add to its relish by placing it in its most sympathetic setting. Yet, he could achieve the discursive in small compass. His talk was never wasteful, but it shaped and decorated its ideas. Some may argue that the best of him was in his talk, full and rounded and rich, afraid of no topic, dismayed by no depths.

There was a third aspect of Ian Mackay which he would, perhaps, have preferred even to the writer or the talker as the remembered Mackay—for he was not covetous of wide fame but preferred the approval of connoisseurs. I am sure he believed that his greatest achievement was the life he led, lived for fifty-four years very fully in the three dimensions of body, head and heart.

Navy-blue Time

BY

NEIL PATERSON

*Neil Paterson, Scots novelist, script-writer and broadcaster, gained the
Atlantic Award in Literature in 1948.*

THERE were many Ian Mackays. The one I knew was
the domesticated animal and must surely have been
the pick of the bunch. The Ian I knew did not eat
daffodils or set his hair alight in the Codgers' Bar. He still
had panache, but it had settled over him like an aura, it
belonged by right, and he did not need to express it outwardly
save in his grizzled halo and an occasional discordant
neck-tie.

I got to know Ian well through broadcasting. I was
resident chairman of a weekly Scottish programme of
unscripted discussion, and Ian, over a couple of years, must
have appeared in this programme a score of times. He greatly
enjoyed broadcasting, especially in Scotland; and that was, I
think, because he knew he was being listened to in Wick.
Wick meant a great deal to him—as much, in a different
way, as Fleet Street did, and I sincerely hope that the town
has followed the example of the street and given him his
immortal place in its annals.

Ian was a natural broadcaster. He had the rare gift of
being able to express himself, of saying and of writing what he
meant. It seemed to me that he spoke as he wrote and wrote
as he spoke, so that the essayist broadcast and the broadcaster wrote essays and the voice in each medium was equally
authentic. It was the real Mackay, and he might have got it
off a Scotch angel. Fallen, he would have me add.

Ian's stories were admirable, and he always had one to fit the occasion. When the programme visited Inverness we were asked whether we believed in the Loch Ness monster. "Of course I believe in the Loch Ness monster," Ian said, "because I am one of the people who invented it." And then he told us, in delectable detail, just how the monster had come into being. He was always on the spot at the time of the fire. His anecdotes, his curious information, his absurd cross-references endeared him to thousands of listeners, and when he broadcast people always wrote asking for more. He had a masterly way of dealing with affectation. If the subject under discussion was at all pretentious, he would merely tilt it up, ever so gently, and expose its backside.

It was always a great joy to the Scottish talks producer, George Runcie, and to me when we had Ian on the programme, for he acted as a kind of catalytic agent, easing the pre-broadcast tensions among strangers and inducing the happy family atmosphere so beloved by all talks producers. Runcie once said to him, "You're better than a tray of drinks, Ian." And Ian said, "That's a particularly odious comparison. I should prefer to be complementary."

The odd thing was that although Ian put us all at ease he was often not at ease himself. When he was uncertain of his listener or himself he would hide his white knuckles inside his sleeves and talk incessantly. It was only after the stranger had shared his delight in his own delightful talk that Ian himself was able to relax. I once saw him talk Douglas Young into an admiring silence, and Douglas is a talker in the Johnsonian tradition, and Scotch forbyes.

One morning after we had been up most of the night arguing about Christianity I noticed at breakfast that Ian was wearing a violently tartan sock on one foot and a sober navy-blue one on the other, and I made some comment. Ian examined his ankles thoughtfully and said at last that this typified his dilemma. "Once upon a time," he said, "I'd have gone through the day with them. Later on, in my middle period, when I'd learned some sense, I would have gone and looked for the other tartan sock. Now I shall go upstairs and put on the other navy-blue one."

I knew Ian in his navy-blue period. I think it was his best time. I'm sure it was his happiest. There were many reasons for that, but the main one was Pat, his wife. When he introduced me to her, Ian said, twinkling, "This is my happy ending," and I thought later, when I saw much of them together, that it was a very happy remark. Ian had approached his marriage with some misgiving, fully aware of the difference in their ages and their backgrounds, and afraid equally of having so valuable a possession and of being possessed. It was a source of continual surprise to him that marriage did not necessarily confine, and that, indeed, his own marriage had broadened him and widened his experience without limiting any of his essential freedoms. He spoke wonderingly about this; and while he explained that this was something quite special, a private triumph that no one else had ever quite pulled off, Pat gleamed demurely and forbore to wink.

They were very happy. One evening when I dropped in on them unexpectedly at their Hampstead flat, Pat was ironing while Ian, in shirt-sleeves—he always took his jacket off whenever he got home—was reading aloud to her from *Man and Superman*. He often read aloud to her, and read beautifully, from the authors he loved best—Shakespeare, Burns, Lear, Housman, delighting to impart and share his own joy, deliberately opening doors in himself for her. They both knew Housman's poetry extremely well, and used it as a private language. "Remarkable," Ian explained, "how satisfactorily one can mutilate the beautiful lines to apply to small domestic trifles." And then the twinkle. "I have a talent for mutilation. Did I ever tell you? . . ." And he would be away again on travels more marvellous than ever Munchausen had and twice as true.

I rarely saw Ian without a book in his pocket. He used always to take a book with him when he left the house, selecting it with meticulous care and then forcing it most brutally into his jacket pocket. It is not the sort of habit that endears a man to his wife, and it precipitated a major domestic crisis, Pat declaring firmly that in future he was to take only small World Classics. Ian said he would take what he liked, and proceeded to discourse on the relative value of a suit and a book. It was a most artful argument, and quite unanswerable. He left the house with *Modern English Short Stories* in his pocket, in the World's Classics edition. "I'm only taking this, mind," he said to me, "because it happens to be the book I wanted anyway. Tomorrow I shall choose precisely what I like."

"Of course he will," said Pat, using me for the ricochet. "That's what I'm saying. He will choose precisely what he likes, out of the World's Classics."

I last saw Ian a day or two before he died. He and Pat and I had just finished dining in a Soho restaurant when someone who knew Ian appeared out of the blue (this was always happening, all over the world) and switched us to a night club where there was an exclusive charity performance and everyone except ourselves was dressed for the occasion. Ian ordered beer: he had drunk nothing else for some years. The waiter raised a supercilious eyebrow.

"*Beer*, sir!"

"Yes," said Ian gently. "It's made from barley and hops, you know. Used to be very fashionable in Egypt about three thousand years ago. Perhaps you could send out for some."

He got his beer.

He was in his best form that night, complimenting Miss Vera Lynn, capping a story of Bernard Braden's. He talked confidently about his future. He was planning a new phase in his life, which had always been his goal but which had not been practicable before. Now, he said, with Pat to hold his hand ("not the one I write with"), he had the sort of home background in which he could really work, and a new, sure sense of direction. He had been under contract for some time to write a life of Ben Tillett. He had been collecting material for years. Now at last he was going to do it. A publisher had asked him to write a book entitled *The English, by a Scot*, and Ian thought that, with application, he could write it in a week or two. ("After all, I've been a chiel among the English for a long time now, and I haven't failed to tak' ma notes.") Another project which was very dear to him and which he talked about enthusiastically that night was a collection of his essays in book form. (How pleased he would have been with that admirable and beautifully produced book of essays, *The Real Mackay*, which the *News Chronicle* published as a memorial to him earlier this year!)

He meant, in future, to do only one essay a week, the Saturday essay in the *News Chronicle*, and, by spending more time on it, to do it better. He hoped to do more public speaking, and more broadcasting. He wanted to break away from being merely "a one paper star turn" and to reach an even wider public.

Listening to him, sharing his excitement, I felt, as Ian himself felt, that his life in letters was just beginning and that the future held boundless possibilities for him. But it was not to be. The beginning was also the end. A few days later he was dead, and it is only, I think, since he died that most of us have realised what great things died with him.

Mackay, the Great Pro

BY

STANLEY BARON

*Stanley Baron, who writes an open-air and many other topics for the
"News Chronicle," is a discerning essayist who was selected by his
newspaper to edit "The Real Mackay," the collection of the columnist's
best work.*

WHAT made Ian tick? What and who for that matter
was Ian Mackay? All of us thought we knew him,
because he had that genius for making anyone he
talked to feel larger and better than life. We wanted to be
sure that we knew him, because that way we were sure he
was right—about us.

I was sure, myself, that I knew Ian well for twenty years.
The very first time we met was on the steps of the old *News
Chronicle* building in Bouverie Street, where another beloved
Scotsman, the late Neil MacIntyre, introduced us. Still more
or less of an *ingénu* in the daily newspaper business, I found
myself at first shaken a bit by the wild tatterdemalion air,
the unspeakable mackintosh. But when I heard what he
said, how sweet it was: so subtly, so delightfully, all about
me and my column. Of course, I knew him—how could it
be otherwise with one who so well knew me!

And then, of course, there were the rigours of war. Many
of us shared those with Ian. The night St. Bride's burned
and we relayed each other from the Press Club bar, taking
peeps to make sure that the steeple still stood. And the
clearing of the dust after the land-mine explosion on Middle
Temple Row—there on a kerb sat Mackay, reading (with
enjoyment but not malice) the scattered secrets from the
little black tins.

Royster-doyster Mackay, man-of-the-people; Mackay the littérateur, the Socialist (but never the politician); the Great Lover Mackay; and (both at the beginning and end of his life, but in different senses) Mackay the Elder Brother—any one of these labels is a perfectly fair one. Evidence for all of them certainly emerged from his work.

After he died the *News Chronicle* decided to publish a selection from everything he had written since he joined the paper in 1934. It fell to me to edit it. A million words is, by any hand, a lot of copy. You need to get the office library files, folder after folder, to realise how much. It was my misfortune, purely in a technical sense, that Ian had laid his large stubby hands on them several times in a manner to make even newspaper librarians cry. Several publishers had at various times tried to get him to make his own selections for reprinting. These upheavals were the result. Nothing ever came of them. Mackay's own verdict, which he pronounced to me several times, was that all good journalism is of its nature ephemeral. So the publishers asked in vain.

Beginning to read, I soon saw two big problems lying ahead. In self-defence so fertile a writer as Ian is bound to develop a formula. There is the engaging start, the fanfare of trumpets, all the tricks of the circus barker designed to get the reader going; then comes the body of the piece; and finally the twist, preferably with a surprise—in Ian's case usually an unexpected turn of phrase crystallising a last-split-second idea. The classic example of this, quoted by Trevor Evans earlier in this book, is the ending of the essay, "No Bones About It." Trying to make a selection in which the repetition of the formula would not be apparent, I then tripped over another difficulty, of which Mackay himself had been all too artfully aware—the brilliant start followed by virtually nothing at all.

It occurred, of course, on those days familiar to all

journalists when not an item of news nor a line of copy of the least interest turned up—not enough to hang even a paragraph on, let alone a column. His room-mates came to dread those days, when Ian would pound his desk, rumple his hair, start fifteen conversations in the hope of provoking some sort of idea—then grimly, as the dead-line of six o'clock approached, begin to write, drawing on his memory, upturning and redressing ideas used before, tearing up six or a dozen false starts before, suddenly, the piece began to flow.

I do not exaggerate in saying that some of his openings on these occasions occupied four-fifths of the whole column and were, as journalism, among the best bits of writing he ever did: brilliant, wildly, fantastically scintillating, just because they were born of desperation.

Such work is the pure product of professionalism: the absolute command of every trick in the trade. Mackay never forgot one of them. All were pressed into use, as necessary, in order to project aspects of his personality. Nor (and he knew it) were all the aspects authentic. No one better enjoyed "acting up"—or more amiably admitted to being found out than Ian.

There was also the trick of the deliberate mistake, used as a sort of insurance policy against the lean days. It seldom failed to work. In would flood the correspondence of scores of readers enjoying the pleasant sensation of being able to correct the Great Mackay—not knowing, in the innocence of their hearts, that this was just what he had intended as a means of getting yet more copy for yet more columns.

In the early days an "inn names" series kept him going, with all manner of variations, for a couple of weeks. A sure sign that he was playing for time, walking round an idea before affixing the half-Nelson, was that splendid old opener, "Not since the days of . . ." None did it better. And then— another sign of the authentic pro—there was that trained card-index mind that enabled him to go straight to the right place among the dozen different reference books that were always on his desk, checking the right allusion.

Ian's reading was vast, but not quite so wide-ranging as the essays might lead you to think. Browsing in The Times Book Club and Simmons' Bookshop on the way to the office, it was the arresting phrase that he was on the lookout for, not always the whole contents of the book. Give him the phrase and it would never be lost. Press the right button years later and out it would come again, falling smoothly into the right place at the right time.

The effect as a rule was one of extraordinary smoothness; but the foreign pieces, clogged with allusions, sometimes suffered by it. Mackay, though an enthusiastic traveller, wrote best at home—and best of all against the clock.

Who and what, then, was the real Mackay?

Superficially a snapper-up of inconsequential trifles, he reveals himself most deeply, for my own money, in almost anything he wrote about his encounters in the worlds of the T.U.C. and politics, and particularly the earlier ones.

This was not just nostalgia or an overdose of reverence for the older Labour leaders. On the death of Frank Hodges, the renegade miners' leader, for instance, he wrote what to me was one of the most telling of all his pieces—no cold analysis but a sensitive and most understanding searching into the heart of a man who had parted from his fellows. With penetration he pointed out that Hodges was a man born out of his time, that had he come up in the modern bureaucratic age of trade unionism he might well have been one of our masters, well paid and well respected. Nor was there any spite in this observation. On the contrary, impelled by loyalty, Ian more than once wrote palpable absurdities, and came near quarrelling with old friends, defending the

STUDY OF IAN

—*by Ronald Searle.*

indefensible in the cause, as he saw it, of his beloved movement.

His awareness of what goes on in the munds of others is shown also in "Mr. Cartwright's Scoop"—crystallising, in eight hundred words, all Fleet Street's shabby splendour, indecorously dying among cigarette ends and the sour smell of beer in a vanished age. Even in such frankly nostalgic writing as "Three Merry Men Go to Paradise" (which was, incidentally, also a "Not since" piece) something more comes out. The three who, in his own phrase, "twinkled into Paradise hand in hand," all having died in the same week-end, were Will Fyffe, George Mozart and George Carney. And though it was Mozart he knew best, it was Carney he most loved, characteristically, for his study of "an ex-officer in a ragged British warm picking up fag-ends in the Mall as a string band playing the *Blue Danube* floated softly from the warm windows of Buckingham Palace." Even in comedy, Ian must have his social irony.

Yet he himself was a hopeless hater. He could bellow, but not bicker. Confronted, even in otherwise congenial company, with anyone he really disliked, he would rather back out than involve himself in dispute. Even then, "a terrible fellow" or "a bad bastard" was as far as he would go in personal criticism.

I have a feeling that behind three-quarters of all Ian wrote was a groping for something of which birth but not life had cheated him. His brother Hughie has told me of the champion Highland piper, the poetess and the branch of the Scottish aristocracy who contributed to his blood, though not to his birth certificate. Ian needed ancestry, yearned for it, and was constantly reclaiming it. When eleven years old he adopted Cockburn into his name; years later he added Marshall. Ian, of course, was merely the Gallic for the John he was born. All three were the reflection of romantic longings. And what he longed for he was determined to get.

The vigour and conscious art with which he put himself over to his reader showed themselves, in embryo, soon after he left Wick. Hughie, who has crippled feet, tells the story of being with Ian in Glasgow. Yearning to dance but too diffident, owing to his disability, to try, he found himself propelled by Ian from one dance hall to another.

"You've *got* to dance," Ian told him. "What's more you've got to make everyone realise you can dance damned well."

Hughie did learn to dance damned well.

Ian did find his ancestors—the shining army of men and women who have written great books, done great deeds and fought for a thousand causes. He claimed them all and by claiming them gained them. But not without craft.

He was a great pro.

Vineyard Valediction

BY

ALEC WAUGH

*Alec Waugh, prolific and versatile author since World War I days,
traveller and club man.*

I DID not meet Ian Mackay until the last fortnight of his
life. But in retrospect that meeting or rather that series of
meetings has a special quality of significance. It was his
last time abroad.

In the last September of 1952 we were both invited to join
a party organised by Gilbey's to visit Bordeaux and attend the
vendange in their vineyards at Château Loudenne. There were
some twenty guests, all of whom were connected in some way
with the Press. Raymond Postgate was there, Pip Youngman
Carter and Cyril Kersh.

It was a three-day trip. We left London on a Thursday
afternoon, spending the night in Paris where we were well
dined and taken afterwards to a cabaret. Very early the next
day we flew down to Bordeaux, to be welcomed there with a
luncheon so worthy of the hospitable traditions of that noble
city that most of us were too drowsy to notice the landscape
closely as we drove in the afternoon past the celebrated
châteaux of the Médoc; several, indeed, did not on arrival
feel equal to a tour of the estate. But Mackay did. He was not
missing anything on the trip, and there was a great deal to
savour and to relish.

Gordon Gilbey, who since World War I has made the
château his special care, acted as our escort. He pointed out
the many changes that had taken place in the production of
wine during the last forty years. The treading of the grapes

has long been abandoned in the Médoc, and now the screw-type hand press has been in its turn replaced by an electrically driven barrel-shaped press that can produce 600 gallons of wine within two hours and the wine is very often shipped to England in tankers instead of casks. There were many changes to be noted, but much that was traditional remained—the women snipping the bunches, the tipping of the large shoulder buckets into the huge tubs that are drawn to the *chais* by dun-coloured, slow-moving oxen—the sacrificial victims of which Vano wrote. Ausonius would not have felt that he was returning to an alien universe could he have strolled that afternoon beside Ian Mackay through the narrow alleys of the vinerows.

At sundown we gathered for cocktails on a stone-flagged terrace. It was a warm, still evening. Loudenne may not be one of the most famous chtâeaux—its wines are classified as a bourgeois growth—but it can provide an ideal setting for a party. Long and low, of faded rose-coloured stone, slate roofed with a rounded tower at each end, it has intrinsic dignity and charm. And there, quarter of a mile away beyond the vines, is the broad, brown historic river with its boats, large and small, plying between Bordeaux and the sea.

The dinner that followed was worthy of the setting. A *cordon bleu* chef and a staff of servants had been requisitioned from Bordeaux. Margaux '75 had been chosen as the "big wine" of the evening, and twelve bottles were opened before Camille Gombeau, the manager, found six that satisfied his exacting standard. The Margaux was preceded by a full-bodied Château Loudenne '24. Raymond Postgate in a summing-up of the evening's wines referred to the Loudenne's "geranium flavour." His was an amusing and erudite disquisition, but the speech of the evening was very definitely Mackay's. Gordon Gilbey in welcoming us had modestly remarked of his own services for the family business that they had not "set the Thames on fire." Mackay caught him up in his reply. "You may not have set the Thames on fire, but thanks to you there is a glow this evening on the Gironde." In that phrase he summed up the essence of a memorable occasion.

Mackay was the *doyen* of the party. But he did not act as though he were. Tall, leonine with his short thick crop of greying hair he was an impressive figure, but he gave himself none of the airs of "a great man." He met everyone upon equal terms, the Gilbey partners, the peasants in the fields, the junior journalists upon the party. He enjoyed every minute of each day, the journey down—even the early start in Paris—the inspection of the cellars, the luncheons and the dinners, the *bal du vendange* in the village when the town hall was crowded, when local dances were performed in local costume, when the bar was supplied with flagons of *gravettes du Médoc* and the last revellers were not home till three. His delight in it all was manifest and contagious.

It was easy to understand during that weekend why Mackay's pen had been devoted to the service of Left Wing causes. Some men become Socialists out of envy, out of jealousy, out of a need for revenge; others through a milk-and-water intellectualism. But Mackay was for the Left out of a love of living; he loved good talk, good company, good food, good wine; he loved his fellow-humans; he wanted them to have their share of those good things and he did not see why they should not. We have reason to be very grateful that fate was generous at the close, allowing him to spend three of his last days in so wholehearted an enjoyment of the things he loved.

Farewell

BY

TREVOR EVANS

T HAT week in Morecambe—the last in his life—Ian
was an obvious choice to respond to the resolution of
thanks to the Press which traditionally ends Labour
Party conferences. This was an occasion which called for a
diplomat as well as an accomplished speaker.

For the week had been one of wounds and bitterness, of
hasty words and chagrined hearts. There were times when a
man's personal affiliations were enough to damn him before
he had uttered his first sentence. There had been that classic
revelation of the unpredictability of the conference when
Dick Crossman, newly elected to the National Executive,
had prefaced his remarks with what he thought was a
witticism only to find it was a fuse which let off a shattering
bomb of anger.

No, that rostrum at Morecambe on the noon of Friday,
October 3rd, 1952, was a place to shun. Yet someone had to
be gracious. And who but Ian for that role? In announcing
that Ian was to reply for the Press, Morgan Phillips described
him as one "who can even make Waterloo Station sound like
a crime thriller." Ian's reply was his swan song. How good
that it should have been such a characteristic reflection of his
warm and understanding personality. Only he would have
dared to risk saucy allusions to the incidents of the stormy
week.

His first sentence was a bull's-eye. "Before I begin," he
announced blandly, "I should like to assure you that I am
not Mark Hewitson." The conference rocked with delight at

this sly repudiation of being a delegate. And to point his moral he had shrewdly chosen the burly and popular Mark Hewitson, a member of the National Executive and a man like himself in build.

Here is the last speech of Ian Mackay, as reported in the official records of the Party:

"Mr. Chairman, your Worship, Mr. Potter" (Mr. W. T. Potter, the railwaymen's leader who had proposed the resolution), "and, if I may use the word without being accused of unprofessional activities, comrades: Waterloo Station is, of course, a crime thriller. One of the first stories I ever wrote was about Waterloo Station, and I was so excited about what I was writing that I began the story like this, 'Three shots rang out in the midnight air—bang! bang!' The readers of the *News Chronicle* are still waiting for the third bang.

"When my colleagues at the Press table asked me if I would reply to this vote of thanks this morning my first impulse was to refuse. My impulse, I can assure you, was not due to any Highland churlishness on my part, or to any hostility to the Labour Party or the Labour movement, to which I must say (without associating the Press table with the statement) I have belonged for many years. I was just a little afraid of making a fool of myself in public. I have always taken the view that it is the function of a newspaper-man not to make speeches himself but to report, and occasionally, with a certain amount of finesse, to misreport the speeches made by other people. But when I considered it a little I thought that, after all, if I did make a fool of myself it would probably not be exceptional. It might not even be noticed on this rostrum.

"I thought, too, that it would be a change to misreport one of my own speeches. Accordingly, I have sent a magnificent oration to the *John O'Groat Journal* in Wick, a speech full of wise saws and scintillating sentences, none of which, I assure you, will I inflict upon you this morning.

"May I say how touching it is at this late stage of the proceedings to be told officially—and I hope that on this issue at least there is no division in the Executive—that we capitalist hacks in the orchestra stalls are fine fellows after all. If the ladies will forgive me for being slightly Anglo-Saxon, it is somewhat refreshing, after having been called bastards for the whole of the week, to be given a certificate of legitimacy at the end of it. We are perhaps not altogether convinced but we are impressed. There has not been such a somersault since St. Paul was on the road to Damascus, or at any rate since the magic midnight that we all remember when the capitalist war turned into a holy crusade.

"This has been a magnificent week from the point of view of the Press, whatever you ladies and gentlemen may think about it. I think all my colleagues, irrespective of political opinions, will be with me when I say that the conduct of the conference by my old friend Harry Earnshaw has been well up to the highest traditions of this great movement. Harry Earnshaw is not what you might call a talkative chap. He and I once sat on the banks of the Danube for six hours and never said a word, which in my case at least borders on the miraculous.

"Harry is a wise leader and a good comrade to everybody, no matter to which side of the movement he may belong. This week he has been the superb conductor of what might be called the Rhapsody in Red. Toscanini himself could not have done better. You must remember that Harry had some tricky scherzos and andantes to conduct, from the graceful Mozartian elegance of Bessie Braddock to that little lullaby for nine anvils which we had from Arthur Deakin the other morning.

"I think I should reveal to you that we are not nearly so

united at the Press table as the members of the Executive on the platform. We have people here from newspapers all over the world, from *Pravda* to the *Poultry World*. Probably I have been selected to do this job because I am something in between—what Kipling would have called a 'bleeding hermaphrodite.' At any rate, my job on the *News Chronicle* is to make the rich red wine of Socialism look like brown cocoa. Sometimes it is rather a difficult job, but at least my Scottish compatriots will realise what I mean when I say that I manage to do it somehow by remembering that in the last resort we are all Jock Tamson's bairns.

"It would be improper of me, representing the Press table, to make any comment at all on your deliberations this week, but I am sure that every one of you, including my friend Nye, will agree in being a little sorry that Herbert Morrison was defeated in the ballot the other day. I am not talking politically, because it would not be proper for me to do so, but I would say that Herbert has been part of the warp and woof of our lives, as well as yours, for so long that it will be rather difficult to look at the platform without him. We wish him good luck, and if I have any knowledge of him at all, his defeat will not mean that we shall not be hearing from him now and again.

"I believe it is customary on these occasions to tell a funny story. I had not one to tell until I met Manny Shinwell who told me a tale new to me about an experience he had when he was Minister of Defence. He has never revealed it so far, but as I am not a politician I am going to take a chance on the Official Secrets Act and tell you what it was.

"An admiral came to him one day and told him he had a ship on the Arctic station, and that the captain had just come back reporting an extraordinary incident in Greenland. He said that at one of the Eskimo stations somebody had told him the Eskimos had a football team. The boys on board ship

had said, 'Well, let's have a crack at them.' So they went to
the field and when they got there they were surprised to find
the team consisted of eight Eskimos, two penguins and a seal.
The game went on and the seal headed the ball all over the
field, while the penguins flipped this way and that way like
Stanley Matthews, with the result that at half-time the score
was: Eskimos five, Britain's Navy nil. While they were having
their lemons, or whatever they have up there during the
interval, the British captain saw an enormous polar bear
coming over an ice floe, and he said, 'Good God, boys! Look
out!' and whipped out his gun and shot the polar bear dead.
Upon which the captain of the Eskimo team said, 'That's
done it. We are not playing any more. That's just the sort of
damn thing the British would do. You've shot the chairman
of our supporters' club.'

"I hope you will excuse me now because I have to go and
write an article on the National Cat Week which opens on
Monday. It is significant, I think—and I hope I shall not be
accused of any kind of political bias in this—that the Cat
Week overlaps, as you might say, the Conservative Party
Conference. But I suppose I can manage to get a look in at
both of them."

. . . . . .

That was his last gift, his legacy, to the Labour Party—the
boom of laughter. And never was it more needed.

Ian stayed only a few minutes down in the bar within the
conference buildings, received the congratulations of all who
saw him, before murmuring to Hugh Chevins, "I think I'll
go out for a breath of fresh air. I've got a bit of a pain here."
And he patted his chest. "Anything wrong with your
ticker?" Chev inquired solicitously. "No," laughed Ian,
"my secret burden is my stomach."

He crossed the road, looked into the Euston Hotel to

inquire if Chevins was there, an odd aberration, seeing he had left Chev in the conference hall only a few minutes earlier. Chev has never ceased to mourn his absence from the hotel at that moment. Ian went to sit down on a bench on the promenade.

A conference delegate, a boiler-maker from Glasgow, passed along the promenade with his wife. He saw and recognised Ian, who was tugging at his collar as if trying to get more air. The boiler-maker plodded on feeling worried. After about a dozen steps he said to his wife, "I wonder if yon Mackay is in trouble?" They turned round and saw Ian stride to the promenade rails, which he gripped. He turned round, with his back to the sea. He collapsed.

When a policeman on point duty raced across the promenade to join the boiler-maker, Ian Mackay was dead.

. . . . . .

Ian had written whimsically, and facetiously, of what he would do with his remains "when the time comes":

"At one time I thought I would have my ashes scattered among the spruce trees on Morven, my boyhood mountain, but then the awful thought occurred to me that I might come back to Fleet Street some day as a roll of newsprint. Then I toyed with the idea of having my ashes secretly poured into the pepper pots at the Carlton Club, but that, I thought, might put some ginger into them. In the end, probably, I shall follow Signor Ubaldi's example and have my bones made into bagpipes. Like most Highlandmen I am a big-boned chap, and they should make several sets of drones and chanters out of me. I can think of no better way than that of having my revenge on this cruel world. So if one night towards the close of the century you hear a pibroch sounding in Piccadilly don't pass by without dropping a coin in the piper's tam o'shanter. He may be playing me."*

* *News Chronicle*, October 21st, 1950.

Index

207